hanley▲wood
HOME BUILDING & REMODELING BASICS

THE ESSENTIAL GUIDE TO

FRAMING

FROM THE EDITORS OF

JLC
The Journal of Light
Construction

hanley▲wood

THE ESSENTIAL GUIDE TO
FRAMING

Published by Hanley Wood
One Thomas Circle, NW, Suite 600
Washington, DC 20005

Distribution Center
29333 Lorie Lane
Wixom, Michigan 48393

THE JOURNAL OF LIGHT CONSTRUCTION
186 Allen Brook Lane
Williston, Vermont 05495

Edited by Clayton DeKorne
Illustrations by Tim Healey
Production by Theresa Emerson
For more information on The Journal of Light Construction or to subscribe to the magazine, visit www.jlconline.com

HANLEY WOOD CONSUMER GROUP
Group Publisher, **Andrew Schultz**
Associate Publisher, Editorial Development, **Jennifer Pearce**
Managing Editor, **Hannah McCann**
Senior Editor, **Nate Ewell**
Proofreader, **Joe Gladziszewski**
Vice President, Retail Sales, **Scott Hill**
National Sales Manager, **Bruce Holmes**

Most Hanley Wood titles are available at quantity discounts with bulk purchases for educational, business,
or sales promotional use. For information, please contact Bruce Holmes at bholmes@hanleywood.com.

VC GRAPHICS
President, Creative Director, **Veronica Claro Vannoy**
Graphic Designer, **Jennifer Gerstein**
Graphic Designer, **Denise Reiffenstein**

PHOTO CREDITS
Front Cover: Getty Images

10 9 8 7 6 5 4 3 2 1

Printed in the United States of America

Library of Congress Control Number: 2005932291

ISBN-10: 1-931131-49-X
ISBN-13: 978-1-931131-49-0

DISCLAIMER OF LIABILITY
Construction is inherently dangerous work and should be undertaken only by trained building professionals. This book is intended for
expert building professionals who are competent to evaluate the information provided and who accept full responsibility for the
application of this information. The techniques, practices, and tools described herein may or may not meet current safety requirements in
your jurisdiction. The editors and publisher do not approve of the violation of any safety regulations and urge readers to follow
all current codes and regulations as well as commonsense safety practices. An individual who uses the information contained in this
book thereby accepts the risks inherent in such use and accepts the disclaimer of liability contained herein.

The editors and publisher hereby fully disclaim liability to any and all parties for any loss, and do not assume any liability whatsoever
for any loss or alleged damages caused by the use or interpretation of the information found in this book, regardless of whether
such information contains deficiencies, errors, or omission, and regardless of whether such deficiencies, errors, or omissions result
from negligence, accident, or any other cause that may be attributed to the editors or publisher.

Acknowledgements

Several years ago, then Journal of Light Construction chief editor Steve Bliss assembled a group of editors to share thoughts on creating our own manual of best practice — the JLC Field Guide. We imagined this as a builder's trusty companion, ever present on the seat of the truck or in the toolbox, ready to answer the kinds of questions that come up on the job site every day.

Thanks to Steve Bliss, who envisioned, mapped, and directed the project in its early stages; to Clayton DeKorne, who expertly executed the work that Steve had started; to Tim Healey for illustration; to JLC staff editors Ted Cushman and Charlie Wardell, who compiled large portions of the original manuscript; to Josie Masterson-Glen for editorial production and copyediting; to Jacinta Monniere for the original book design; to Barb Nevins, Lyn Hoffelt, and Theresa Emerson for production work; to Ursula Jones for production support; and to Sal Alfano and Rick Strachan of Hanley Wood's Washington, D.C., office for executive management.

Finally, special thanks to all the authors and JLC editors over the years, too numerous to mention, whose work is the basis of this volume.

Don Jackson
JLC Editor

Introduction

Over the last 20 years, The Journal of Light Construction has amassed a wealth of first-hand, practical building knowledge from professionals who have dedicated themselves to custom residential projects. In the Home Building & Remodeling Basics Series, we have distilled this valuable knowledge into handy reference guides — selecting the critical data, fundamental principles, and rules of thumb that apply to strategic phases of residential building and remodeling.

Our intention is not to set building standards, but to provide the housebuilding trades with a compilation of practical details and proven methods that work for the many builders, remodelers, subcontractors, engineers, and architects who are committed to producing top-quality, custom homes. The recommendations we have compiled in these volumes usually exceed the building code. Code compliance is essential to building a safe home — one that won't collapse or create unsafe living conditions for the occupants. However, we are striving to reach beyond this minimum standard by offering a record of best practice for residential construction: details and methods used not only to produce a safe building, but to create a long-lasting, fine-quality home.

While it is not our first focus, we have made every effort to uphold the building codes. The prescriptive recommendations in this book are generally consistent with the 2000 International Residential Code and the Wood Frame Construction Manual for One- and Two-Family Dwellings, published by the American Forest and Paper Association. Although these standards reflect the major U.S. model codes (CABO, BOCA, ICBO, and SBCCI), regional conditions have forced some municipalities to adopt more stringent requirements. Before taking the information in this volume as gospel, consult your local code authority.

As comprehensive as we have tried to make this resource, it will be imperfect. Certainly we have strived to limit any error. However, many variables, not just codes, affect local building and remodeling practices. Climate variability, material availability, land-use regulations, and native building traditions all impact how houses are built in each city, town, county, and region. To account for every variation would require a database of understanding far greater than the scope of this book. Instead, we focus here on some principles of physics, design, and craftsmanship that won't change by region or style. It is our hope that these principles, used alongside the building code, will guide professionals toward a greater understanding of best practice.

Clayton DeKorne

Editor

How to Use this Book

This volume is intended to be used as a reference book for professionals and experienced homeowners with an understanding of basic construction techniques. It is organized in general order of construction, and within each section we have provided several navigational tools to help you quickly located the information you need, including a section headline at the top of the page, cross-references within the text, and references to Figures and illustrations.

Table of Contents: The two-page table of contents found on the following spread offers a detailed look at this book — featuring not just each section, but the individual topics found therein, along with page numbers for quick reference.

Index: A detailed index of the entire volume can be found at the back of this book.

Figures: When appropriate, tables, graphs, and illustrations have been added to help clarify the subject matter. Every effort has been made to place these Figures on the same page, or spread of pages, as the copy which references them. You will find references to Figures in bold in the text; in the event that the Figure falls on an earlier page or in another section, a page reference will be included in the text.

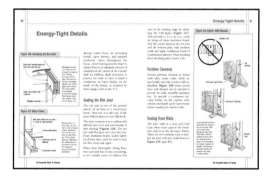

Be sure to pick up the other three books in the Home Building & Remodeling Basics Series for more valuable information that will help you get your next project done right:

- The Essential Guide to Roofing
- The Essential Guide to Exteriors
- The Essential Guide to Foundations

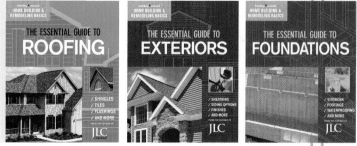

Table of Contents

Estimating Materials

Converting Linear Feet to Board-Feet

Formula method. To find board-feet, multiply the total length (in ft.) by the nominal lumber thickness by the width (in in.), and then divide the total by 12. For example: (10) 8-ft. 2x4s = (80 x 2 x 4) ÷ 12 = 53.3 board-feet

$$(L \times T \times W) \div 12$$

Factor method. Alternatively, use the conversion factors in **Figure 1**.

Floors and Ceilings

Estimating Number of Joists

To calculate the number of joists, use the formulas shown in **Figure 2** for the appropriate on-center spacing.

Estimating Rim Joists

Remember to include rim stock in the total joist count. Rim joist stock is calculated as follows:

BUILDING LENGTH (FT.) x 2/
LUMBER LENGTH

Figure 1. Linear Feet to Board-Feet Conversion

Nominal Lumber Size	Conversion Factor
1x4	.33333
1x6	.50000
1x8	.66667
1x10	.833333
1x12	1.00000
2x3	.50000
2x4	.666667
2x6	1.00000
2x8	1.33333
2x10	1.66667
4x4	1.33333
4x6	2.00000
6x6	3.00000

As an alternative method of calculating board-feet, multiply the lin. ft. of each lumber size you are using by the corresponding conversion factor. Example: (10) 8-ft. 2x4s = 80 x .666667 = 53.3 board-feet

Lumber lengths should be multiples of the o.c. spacing. For example, use 12s, 16s, 20s, etc., for 16-in. o.c. joist spacing. Depending on the length of the building, it may be more efficient to count these individually, mixing lumber lengths that break evenly on the joists.

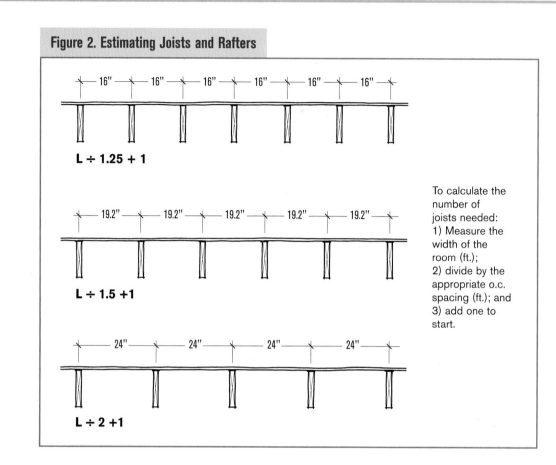

Figure 2. Estimating Joists and Rafters

L ÷ 1.25 + 1

L ÷ 1.5 +1

L ÷ 2 +1

To calculate the number of joists needed:
1) Measure the width of the room (ft.);
2) divide by the appropriate o.c. spacing (ft.); and
3) add one to start.

Estimating Subflooring

The most accurate method of estimating subflooring is to graph scaled lines over the floor plans in 4x8-ft. increments. For a quick alternative, calculate as follows:

- For each section of subfloor, square off any jogs or cantilevers from the outside perimeter on the plans to form one large perimeter rectangle.

- For each section, multiply the length by the width of the perimeter rectangle.

- Divide by 32 (for 4x8 panels).

$$\text{FLOOR AREA} = \text{LENGTH x WIDTH}$$

$$\text{SHEATHING (4x8 PANELS)} = \text{FLOOR AREA} \div 32$$

Remember to add a couple of sheets to the total panel count to accommodate cutting error and waste, especially if there are jogs in the floor plan.

Walls

Estimating Plate Stock

Order wall plates in a quantity that's at least four times the total length of the walls. On walls that run in the same direction as the trusses or joists, an additional plate is needed for drywall backing at the ceiling. More will be needed to cover waste, miscellaneous backing, and continuous fire blocking for walls over 8 ft. high.

Estimating Studs

For a small house (less than 2,000 sq. ft.) with 16-in. o.c. framing, order 1 stud for each lin. ft. of wall framing — both interior and exterior. For a larger house framed 16 in. o.c., order 1.25 studs for each lin. ft. of wall framing.

Estimating Headers

In a house with windows under 36 in. wide, use the following shortcuts:

For solid-sawn headers:

1) Count the number of windows and doors; count French doors or sliders as 2;

2) Divide by 3 and order that many 10-footers.

For doubled-2x headers:

1) Count the number of windows and doors; count French doors or sliders as 2;

2) Multiply by 2;

3) Divide by 3 and order that many 10-footers.

For extra large or extra narrow windows, calculate headers individually.

Estimating Wall Sheathing

For rectangular wall areas:

$$\text{WALL AREA} = \text{TOTAL WALL LENGTH} \times \text{WALL HEIGHT}$$

$$\text{SHEATHING (4x8 PANELS)} = \text{WALL AREA} \div 32$$

1) Multiply the total length of exterior walls by the wall height to get total wall area;

2) Subtract the areas of major openings such as sliders or large windows;

3) Divide by 32 (for 4x8 panels).

Remember to account for gable-end walls.

For regular gables (same pitch both sides of ridge):

Multiply span by total rise. This gives you the total for two gable-ends.

For irregular gables or single gable-end walls:

1) Multiply total run by total rise for each gable end;

2) Divide by 32.

Figure 3. Rafter Line Length (LL) Ratios

Roof Pitch/12	COM LL Ratio	H/V LL Ratio	Roof Pitch/12	COM LL Ratio	H/V LL Ratio
1	1.0035	1.4167	8	1.2019	1.5635
1½	1.0078	1.4197	8½	1.2254	1.5817
2	1.0138	1.4240	9	1.2500	1.6008
2½	1.0215	1.4295	9½	1.2754	1.6207
3	1.0308	1.4361	10	1.3017	1.6415
3½	1.0417	1.4440	10½	1.3288	1.6630
4	1.0541	1.4530	11	1.3566	1.6853
4½	1.0680	1.4631	11½	1.3851	1.7083
5	1.0833	1.4743	12	1.4142	1.7321
5½	1.1000	1.4866	14	1.5366	1.8333
6	1.1180	1.5000	16	1.6667	1.9437
6½	1.1373	1.5144	18	1.8028	2.0616
7	1.1577	1.5298	24	2.2361	2.4495
7½	1.1792	1.5462			

To convert Rafter Run to Line Length:

1) Select LL ratio for given slope in table above;

2) Multiply rafter run by LL ratio.

To find Full Rafter Length (add for any overhang at the eaves):

1) Multiply the horizontal length of overhang by the same LL ratio;

2) Add this overhang length to the rafter LL.

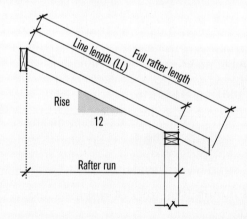

When estimating rafter lengths and calculating spans, convert the rafter run (horizontal distance) to a sloped distance (line length) using these ratios.

Examples: On a 6/12 roof with a run* of 15 ft., find the net rafter length for the common rafters: 15 ft. x 1.118 = 16.77 ft. or 16 ft. 9¼ in. Round up to the next 2-ft. increment for the lumber length needed (18-footers).

If the roof has a 16-in. overhang, measured along the rafter, the job will require 20-ft. rafters: 16 in. x 1.118 = 1.491 ft. + 16.77 ft. = 18.261 ft. or 18 ft. 3¼ in. Round up to 20-footers.

* For more precise calculations of rafters, use an *effective run*, which is shortened for the ridge thickness. For more information, see *A Roof Cutter's Secrets to Framing the Custom Home* (JLC Books)

Roofs

Estimating Rafter Length

To find the full rafter length, multiply the correct line length ratio in **Figure 3** by the horizontal run of the rafter. This gives the net rafter length, or line length, from top plate to ridge. Then add for the plumb cut at the ridge and overhang to find the full rafter length.

Estimating Number of Common Rafters

To calculate the number of common rafters, use the formulas provided in **Figure 2** (page 2) for the appropriate on-center spacing.

Remember to include ridge stock.

Estimating Hip and Valley Rafter Lengths

To calculate the length of each hip rafter, use the Hip/Valley LL ratio shown in **Figure 3**.

Estimating Jack Rafters

For a simple hip or valley, each pair of jack rafters is equal in length to one common (one long jack + one short jack = one common).

Estimating Roof Sheathing

$$\text{ROOF AREA} = \begin{array}{l}\text{PERIMETER WALL} \\ \text{LENGTHS (INCL. OVER HANGS)} \\ \text{x RAFTER LINE LENGTH}\end{array}$$

$$\text{SHEATHING (4x8 PANELS)} = \text{ROOF AREA} \div 32$$

1) Add overhang distance to exterior wall lengths;

2) Multiply the total length of the perimeter (wall length + overhang) by the rafter line length (**Figure 3**) to get total roof area (on gable roofs, don't include the gable-end wall in the total length);

3) Divide by 32 (for 4x8 panels).

Calculate roofs of different pitches individually.

Remember to add a couple of sheets to the total to account for error and waste.

Selecting Lumber

Selecting Dimensional Lumber

Dimensional lumber is differentiated by several species groups. The main species groups in the U.S. are Spruce-Pine-Fir (Canadian), Douglas Fir-Larch, Hem-Fir, and Southern Pine (typically pressure-treated). Each species group is available in a number of grades, but unless otherwise

Figure 4. Strength of Wood

		Design Values[1] for 2x8 (Nominal) Lumber	
Species Group	**Grade**	**Extreme Fiber Stress in Bending (Fb)[2]**	**Modulus of Elasticity (E)[3]**
D-Fir-L	Select Strength	1,620	1.9
	No. 1/ No. 2	1,020	1.6
	No.3	570	1.4
SPF	Select Strength	1,500	1.5
	No. 1/ No. 2	1,050	1.4
	No. 3	600	1.2
Hem-Fir	Select Strength	1,560	1.7
	No. 1/ No. 2	1,200	1.6
	No.3	690	1.4
SYP	Select Strength	2,300	1.8
	No. 1	1,500	1.7
	No. 2	1,200	1.6
	No. 3	600	1.4

(1) These values include a size factor for 8-inch-wide nominal members used in normal conditions (lumber with a moisture content <= 19% placed on edge). Wet lumber or flat members require higher values. (2) psi (3) million psi

This table shows comparative design values for the four main wood species used in this manual. The values assume the lumber will be loaded on the edge. Extreme fiber stress in bending (Fb) is a measure of the lumber's strength to resist loads applied perpendicular to the grain. This load produces **tension** in the wood fibers along the edge farthest from the applied load, and **compression** in the fibers along the edge nearest to the load. The Modulus of Elasticity (E) is a ratio of the amount the wood will **deflect** in proportion to the applied load. **E is a measure of stiffness, whereas Fb is a measure of strength.**

Figure 5. Predicted Shrinkage of Dimension Lumber

Lumber Size	Actual Width	Width @ 19% MC (at Delivery)	Width @ 11% MC (Humid Climates)	Width @ 8% MC (Average Climates)	Width @ 6% MC (Arid Climates)
2x4	3¹/₂"	3¹/₂"	3⁷/₁₆"	3³/₈"	3³/₈"
2x6	5¹/₂"	5¹/₂"	5³/₈"	5⁵/₁₆"	5⁵/₁₆"
2x8	7¹/₂"	7¹/₄"	7¹/₈"	7¹/₁₆"	7"
2x10	9¹/₄"	9¹/₄"	9¹/₁₆"	9"	8¹⁵/₁₆"
2x12	11¹/₄"	11¹/₄"	11"	10¹⁵/₁₆"	10⁷/₈"

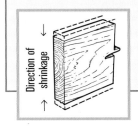

Direction of shrinkage

Framing lumber shrinks primarily across its width; shrinkage from end to end is insignificant. Actual shrinkage varies depending on the lumber's moisture content when delivered and the area's climate.

specified, most framing lumber is #2. Lower grades may be allowed for studs (Stud-Grade) and top plates (Utility-Grade).

Strength values for these and other North American species and species groups are shown in **Figure 4**. For convenience, the span tables in this book (pages 94-117) are listed by species group. If a species or group is not listed in the charts, use the spans for a species or group with the same or higher Fb value.

Shrinkage

Kiln-dried lumber is stamped K-D (kiln-dried) or S-Dry (surface dry), and is shipped with a moisture content of about 19%. Anything larger than a 6x6 is generally not available K-D.

In a completed building, framing eventually dries to an average of 6% to 11% moisture content, depending on climate. This drying causes the lumber to shrink across the grain; shrinkage along the grain is negligible. **Figure 5** shows the degree of shrinkage in flat-sawn framing lumber. Shrinkage in large carrying beams can cause one part of a house to settle more than others, causing drywall cracks and other problems (**Figure 6**).

However, using flush beams with hangers, or engineered lumber or steel, can reduce the potential for shrinkage problems. If dimensional

Figure 6. Avoiding Cumulative Shrinkage

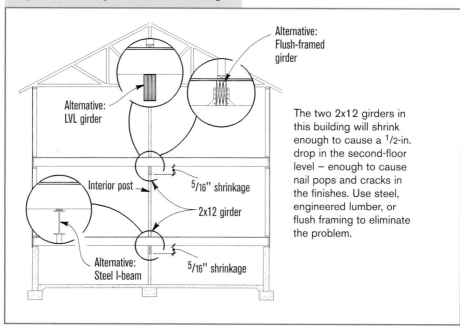

Alternative: Flush-framed girder

Alternative: LVL girder

Interior post

5/16" shrinkage

2x12 girder

Alternative: Steel I-beam

5/16" shrinkage

The two 2x12 girders in this building will shrink enough to cause a 1/2-in. drop in the second-floor level — enough to cause nail pops and cracks in the finishes. Use steel, engineered lumber, or flush framing to eliminate the problem.

Figure 7. Flushed-Framed Floor Joists

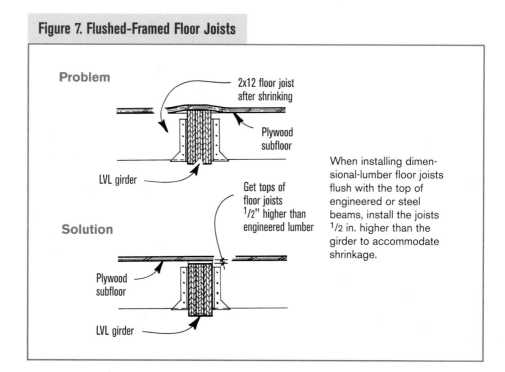

Problem

2x12 floor joist after shrinking

Plywood subfloor

LVL girder

Solution

Get tops of floor joists 1/2" higher than engineered lumber

Plywood subfloor

LVL girder

When installing dimensional-lumber floor joists flush with the top of engineered or steel beams, install the joists 1/2 in. higher than the girder to accommodate shrinkage.

lumber is hung flush from a beam made of steel or engineered lumber, the result can be a bulge at the beam (see **Figure 7**).

Selecting Sheathing and Subfloor Panels

Sheathing and subflooring should consist of performance-rated structural panels. These are made from plywood or oriented-strand board (OSB), and should carry a stamp (**Figure 8**) from APA-The Engineered Wood Association (formerly the American Plywood Association).

Panel Use Ratings

For framing, choose only from the following panel grades:

- **Sheathing** panels are designed for use on roof decks and walls;

- **Structural 1** panels are designed for use on shear walls;

- **Sturdi-Floor®** tongue-and-groove panels are designed for use as subflooring.

Panel Exposure Ratings

For framing, select panels with only the following exposure ratings:

- **Exterior** panels can be used outdoors;

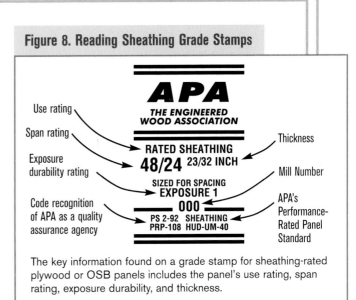

Figure 8. Reading Sheathing Grade Stamps

Use rating

Span rating

Exposure durability rating

Code recognition of APA as a quality assurance agency

APA
THE ENGINEERED WOOD ASSOCIATION

RATED SHEATHING
48/24 23/32 INCH

SIZED FOR SPACING
EXPOSURE 1
000
PS 2-92 SHEATHING
PRP-108 HUD-UM-40

Thickness

Mill Number

APA's Performance-Rated Panel Standard

The key information found on a grade stamp for sheathing-rated plywood or OSB panels includes the panel's use rating, span rating, exposure durability, and thickness.

- **Exposure 1** panels can withstand moisture during normal construction delays — up to a full season, according to APA. However, the panels should be covered up as soon as possible.

Other exposure ratings for wood panels include:

- **Exposure 2** panels are typically used for protected construction and industrial applications where the potential for high humidity and water leakage may exist for limited times;

- **Interior panels** are made with water-soluble interior-grade glues and are intended for interior applications only, not for framing.

Panel Span Ratings

Span ratings on sheathing grade stamps may have two numbers such as

24/16. The first indicates the allowable roof span (in this case, 24 in. o.c.) and the second indicates the subflooring span (16 in. o.c.). Span ratings for multipurpose panels are: 24/0, 24/16, 32/16, 40/20, and 48/24.

If a sheathing panel stamp includes only one span number, the panel is for use on walls only.

Sturdi-Floor® panels are engineered for use as subflooring. They have span ratings of 16-, 20-, 24-, 32-, and 48-in.

Panel Thickness

Plywood and OSB are always $1/32$ in. smaller than their nominal sizes. For example, $1/2$-in. plywood actually measures only $15/32$ in.

Roof Panel Span

Roof panels should be a minimum of $1/2$ in. thick for 16-in. o.c. framing, and $5/8$ in. thick for 24-in. o.c. framing.

For roofs framed 24-in. o.c., use H-clips to support the edges of the sheathing at mid-span. Clips create the proper gap and help stiffen panel edges.

OSB

While the strength and nail-holding ability of OSB and plywood are equal for similarly rated panels, OSB swells more when wet. Because of this, some builders avoid OSB in subflooring, especially in kitchens or baths, where exposure to wet conditions is likely. Some flooring contractors will not install hardwood flooring over OSB subflooring, although tests have shown that it performs the same as plywood in this application. OSB is not considered a suitable underlayment for use directly under ceramic tile or resilient flooring, however.

Unused OSB should be stored under cover on the job site. If an installed OSB subfloor is left uncovered for a long period after installation, consider treating it with a water repellent.

Selecting Engineered Lumber

Engineered studs and beams are not direct substitutes for solid lumber. Each engineered product has special installation requirements. Be sure to consult the product's technical literature before using any new engineered product.

Most engineered lumber is made with exterior glue. The glue will hold up under normal construction delays, but it is not waterproof. Therefore, all engineered lumber should be protected from the weather on-site and stored flat.

Wood I-Joists

Using wood I-joists places the strongest material (typically LVL) where the bending stresses are greatest — in the *flanges* along the top and bottom of the beam. This lets the lightweight beams span great distances with minimal deflection, providing a very stiff floor.

I-joist webs consist of plywood or OSB, making them more susceptible to water damage than sawn lumber. Therefore, I-joists must be stored under cover — particularly those with OSB webs. Care must be taken when drilling or notching the webs to allow mechanicals to pass through (see "Boring and Notching I-Joists," page 31).

Engineered Studs

For tall walls and kitchen walls that must remain straight for countertop and cabinet runs, engineered studs are a cost-effective alternative to dimensional lumber. Follow manufacturers' guidelines for installing specific products. General use precautions are shown in **Figure 9**.

Finger-jointed studs aren't any stronger than dimensional lumber of the same species, but because the defects have been cut out, they are more dimensionally stable. In addition, the grain is interrupted by glue joints, making finger-jointed studs less likely to twist and bow.

The glue that holds the joints together is water-resistant, but these studs should be protected from prolonged exposure to the weather.

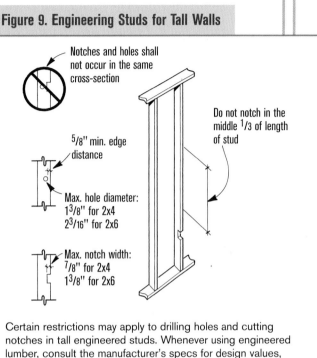

Figure 9. Engineering Studs for Tall Walls

Notches and holes shall not occur in the same cross-section

Do not notch in the middle $1/3$ of length of stud

$5/8"$ min. edge distance

Max. hole diameter: $1^{3}/8"$ for 2x4 $2^{3}/16"$ for 2x6

Max. notch width: $7/8"$ for 2x4 $1^{3}/8"$ for 2x6

Certain restrictions may apply to drilling holes and cutting notches in tall engineered studs. Whenever using engineered lumber, consult the manufacturer's specs for design values, load tables, and nailing requirements.

Laminated Strand Lumber (LSL). LSL is made from strands of wood bonded with a polyurethane adhesive, and it is used mostly for rim boards, studs, and headers. LSL studs are straight and true, but heavier than solid lumber. They have sharp edges so wear gloves when handling. LSL studs take air nails about the same way dimensional lumber does, but there are fewer problems with splits if nails are kept at least $1/2$ in. from the edges.

Engineered Beams

Engineered beams may consist of laminated veneer lumber (LVL), glue-laminated timbers (glulams), or parallel-strand lumber (Parallam®). Be aware that the large loads carried by an engineered beam will concentrate at the bearing points. To keep the beam's fibers from crushing under the weight, be sure to allow sufficient bearing surface. Installation of large engineered beams may require a crane or lift.

Laminated-Veneer Lumber (LVL). LVL is a strong, versatile, engineered product that resembles plywood. LVL beams are typically built up from several LVL members nailed or bolted together. Bolting is preferable where the beam is side-loaded (e.g., a floor system with flush framing) or where it will be exposed to the weather. Side loading with joist hangers can cause the outer LVL members to "peel off" if they are not bolted together.

Before ordering LVL, it's important to note the grade, species, and manufacturer specified by the designer. For example, Douglas-fir LVL is somewhat weaker than yellow-pine LVL. While most LVL has a water-resistant coating, it is still vulnerable to cupping when exposed to moisture. So store it dry.

Glue-Laminated Timbers (glulams). A glulam consists of dimension lumber face-laminated with structural adhesives. Three appearance grades are available — industrial, architectural, and premium. Design values are the same for all three grades, but the better grades have fewer surface defects. This is important in residential construction where most glulams are left exposed.

Glulams come in widths ranging from $2^1/2$ to $10^3/4$ in. Depths are multiples of the lamination thickness. For example, a glulam with eight $1^1/2$-in. laminations will be 12 in. deep.

Most glulams are delivered in a wrapping that protects the surface of any exposed beam during shipping and installation. If possible, don't remove this wrapping until all interior finishing is complete. Protect wrapping so that water doesn't leak in and become trapped.

Never notch or drill a glulam without consulting either the fabricator or a structural engineer. Connections should be made so that the beam can swell and shrink with moisture swings.

Parallel-Strand Lumber (Parallam®). Sold under the brand name Parallam®, this product consists of strands of veneer that are aligned, coated with glue, and cured with a combination of pressure and microwaves. The resulting beam is stronger and stiffer than solid-sawn lumber and is equivalent in strength to multiple LVLs. However, you save the expense of bolting and don't need to worry about side loading or warping from moisture. The material is somewhat harder to cut and nail than solid lumber.

Nails

Holding Power of Nails

A nail's holding power is a function of its diameter, how far it penetrates the wood, and the type of wood it penetrates. In framing, nails should never be loaded in withdrawal (where the load acts parallel to the nail shank and tries to pull it out). Instead, framing nails should be loaded only laterally (where the load acts perpendicular to the shank). Also, nails have more holding power when driven into the side grain rather than into the end grain. In fact, nailing into the end grain will reduce a nail's lateral load capacity by approximately one-third.

Figure 10. Lateral Strength of Common vs. Box Nails

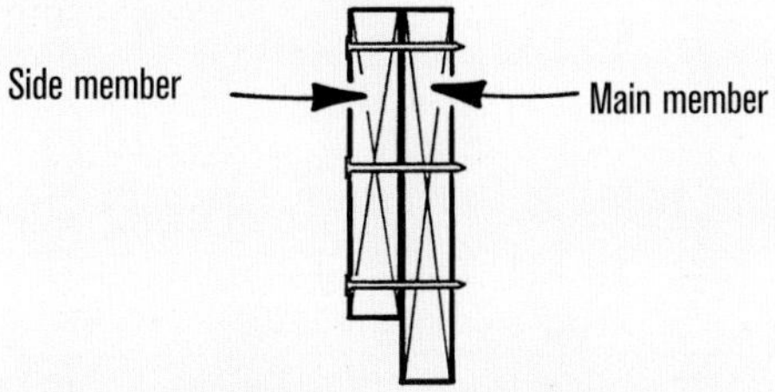

Side member → ← Main member

Penny Wt.	8d		10d		12d		16d		20d	
Nail Type	Common	Box	Common	Box	Common	Box	Common	Box	Common	Box
Diameter (in.)	0.131	0.113	0.148	0.128	0.148	0.128	0.162	0.135	0.192	0.148
Side Member Thickness (in.)	0-3/4		0-3/4		0-3/4		1 1/2		1 1/2	
Lateral Rating (lb.)										
SPF	70	57	83	68	83	68	120	88	144	100
D-F-L	90	72	105	87	105	87	141	103	170	118
Hem-Fir	73	58	85	70	85	70	122	89	147	102
SYP	104	79	121	101	121	101	154	113	185	128

Nails are rated for "lateral capacity," which is greatly affected by the nail's diameter. Since box nails are skinnier than commons, they have lower strength values. The values shown vary with the type of framing lumber used, and they assume the nail will penetrate the main member (illustration at top) at least 12 diameters.

Box vs. Common Nails

Lateral strength is largely a function of a nail's diameter and the density of the type of wood into which the nail is driven. For example, 10d and 12d nails have the same diameter and the same lateral strength in each type of wood.

Common nails are stronger than box nails because of their greater diameter (**Figure 10**).

When substituting box for common nails, calculate the nail size needed using the conversion ratios shown in **Figure 11**.

Figure 11. Conversion Ratio for Common to Box Nails

To convert required number of common nails of a given size to box nails, multiply by the appropriate ratio and round up.

Penny Wt.	8d	10d	12d	16d	20d
Ratio	1.23	1.22	1.22	1.36	1.44

S-P-F lumber assumed.

Do not substitute a common nail that's specified on the plans for an equal number of box nails. Instead, multiply the specified number of common nails by the conversion ratio shown in the chart and round up to find the equivalent number of box nails.

Withdrawal Strength of Nails

Nails are much stronger when loaded laterally (across the nail) than when loaded in withdrawal (along the length of the nail). Withdrawal from end grain is particularly weak and not accepted as a structural connection by most codes. Withdrawal values from sidegrain are given in **Figure 12**.

Figure 12. Withdrawal Strength Design Values of Common vs. Box Nails

Penny Wt.	8d		10d		12d		16d		20d	
Nail Type	Common	Box	Common	Box	Common	Box	Common	Box	Common	Box
Diameter (in.)	0.131	0.113	0.148	0.128	0.148	0.128	0.162	0.135	0.192	0.148
Withdrawal Value*										
SPF	21	18	23	20	23	20	26	21	30	23
D-F-L	32	28	36	31	36	31	40	33	47	36
Hem-Fir	22	19	25	21	25	21	27	23	32	25
SYP	41	35	46	40	46	40	50	42	59	46

* psi per inch of penetration into side grain of main member

This table shows the allowable load values for typical common and box nails. These values represent the pounds per square inch of load applied per penetration into the side grain of the main member.

Toenails

For toenails loaded in withdrawal, multiply the values in **Figure 12** by .67. For toenails loaded laterally, multiply the values in **Figure 10** by .83. Toenails should be driven at an angle of about 30 degrees from the face of the stud or other member being attached (**Figure 13**).

Pneumatic Nails

Pneumatic nails are typically sold by a specified shank diameter in inches (.120, .131, and .148 are common for framing nails). These are typically skinnier than common nails of equal length and, therefore, have lower lateral strength (**Figure 14**) and withdrawal values (**Figure 15**). Consult manufacturers for lateral strength of specific nail types.

Galvanized Nails

Galvanized nails are made from zinc-coated steel. The zinc protects the steel from rust. How well a nail resists rust depends on the amount of zinc and how it's applied.

Hot-dipped nails (coated by immersion in molten zinc) are the most durable.

Figure 13. Proper Toenailing

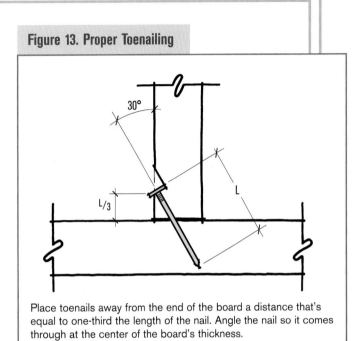

Place toenails away from the end of the board a distance that's equal to one-third the length of the nail. Angle the nail so it comes through at the center of the board's thickness.

Figure 14. Lateral Strength of Air Nails

Nail Diameter	Wood Species			
	SPF	DFL	Hem-Fir	SYP
0.12"	19	29	20	37
0.131"	21	32	22	41
0.148"	23	36	25	46
0.162"	26	40	27	50

Values are based on a 10-year "normal" load duration, and assume: 1) smooth-shank nails driven perpendicular to the wood grain; and 2) both side and main members are of the same wood species. When toenailing, multiply the values by .83, as described in "Toenails," top of page.

Figure 15. Withdrawal Strength Load Values for Air Nails

Nail Length	Nail Dia.	Wood Species			
		SPF	**DFL**	**Hem-Fir**	**SYP**
2 1/2"	0.131"	52	62	54	67
3"	0.12"	69	81	71	89
3"	0.131"	79	93	80	101
3"	0.148"	84	99	86	109
3 1/4"	0.12"	69	81	71	89
3 1/4"	0.131"	79	93	80	101
3 1/2"	0.162"	92	109	94	119

Withdrawal values (psi per inch of penetration into the main member) are based on a 10-year "normal" load duration, and assume: 1) smooth-shank nails driven perpendicular to the wood grain; and 2) both side and main members are of the same wood species. When toenailing, multiply the values by .83, as described in "Toenails," previous page.

Hot-galvanized (HG) nails are coated with zinc chips in a hot tumbler, a process that can leave an uneven coating. A certain percentage of these nails will rust when used outside.

Electroplated nails are smooth and shiny, but the thin zinc coating will oxidize away quickly when exposed. This makes them a poor choice for exterior work.

Mechanical plated, or "peen" plated, nails have a zinc layer that isn't as thick as that used on a hot-dipped nail, so it is less corrosion-resistant. However, mechanical plating is appropriate for screws as the thin coating won't clog the threads.

Figure 16. Nailing Schedules

Roof Framing	Number of Common Nails	Number of Air Nails
Rafter to top plate (toe-nailed)[1]	3-8d per rafter	3-3 x .131 per rafter
Ceiling joist to top plate (toe-nailed)[1]	3-16d per joist	5-3 x .131 per rafter
Ceiling joist to parallel rafter (face-nailed)[1][2]	3-16d per joist	4-3 x .131[1] per rafter
Ceiling joist laps over partitions (faced-nailed)	3-16d per lap	4-3 x .131 per rafter
Collar tie to rafter (face-nailed)[1]	3-16d per joist[1][2]	4-3 x .131 per rafter
Blocking to rafter (toe-nailed)	2-8d each end	2-3 x .131 each end
Roof rafter to ridge beam[1]	3-10d per rafter	3-3 x .131 per rafter
Jack rafter to hip (toe-nailed)	3-10d per rafter	3-3 x .131 per rafter
Roof Sheathing[1]		
Structural panels	1-8d every 6 in. edge, 12 in. field	1-2 1/2 x .131 every 6 in. edge, 12 in. field

Figure 16. Nailing Schedules, continued

Wall Framing	Number of Common Nails	Number of Air Nails
Top or bottom plate to stud (end-nailed)[1]	2-16d per stud	3-3 x .131 per stud
	3-16d per 2x6 stud	4-3 x .131 per stud
Top or bottom plate to stud (toe-nailed)[1]	3-16d per stud	4-3 x .131 per stud
	4-16d per 2x6 stud	
	5-16d per stud	3-3 x .131 per stud
Top plate to top plate (face-nailed)[1]	2-16d every 16 in.	2-3 x .131 every 12 in.
Top plates at intersections (face-nailed)	2-16d each side of joint	4-3 x .131 each side of joint
Stud to stud (face-nailed)	2-16d every 24 in.	2-3 x .131 every 16 in.
Header to header (face-nailed)	1-16d every 16 in. along edges	1-3 x .131 every 12 in. along edges
Bottom plate to floor joist, band joist, end joist, or blocking (face-nailed)[3][4]	1-16d every 16 in.	1-3 x .131 every 8 in. along edges
Wall Sheathing[1]		
Structural panels	1-8d every 6 in. edge, 12 in. field	1-2½ x .131 every 6 in. edge, 12 in. field
Floor Framing		
Joist to sill, top plate or girder (toe-nailed)	4-8d per joist	4-3 x .131 per joist
Bridging to joist (toe-nailed)	2-8d each end	2-2½ x .131 each end
Blocking to joist (toe-nailed)	2-8d each end	2-2½ x .131 each end
Blocking to sill or top plate (toe-nailed)	3-16d each block	4-3 x .131 each block
Ledger strip to beam (face-nailed)	3-16d below each joist	4-3 x .131 below each joist
Joist on ledger to beam (toe-nailed)	3-8d per joist	3-3 x .131 per joist
Rim joist to joist (end-nailed)	3-16d per joist	4-3 x .131 per joist
Rim joist to sill or top plate (toe-nailed)[1]	2-16d every 12 in.	2-3 x .131 every 8 in.
Floor Sheathing		
Structural panels		
1 in. or less	1-8d every 6 in. edge, 12 in. field	1-2½ x .131 every 6 in. edge, 12 in. field
Greater than 1 in.	1-10d every 6 in. edge, 6 in. field	1-3¼ x .131 every 6 in. edge, 6 in. field

(1) For high wind areas, consult local codes.
(2) See **Figure 87**, page 53, for detailed schedules to accommodate specific roof loading conditions.
(3) Nailing requirements are based on wall sheathing nailed 6 in. o.c. at the panel edge. If wall sheathing is nailed 3 in. o.c. at the panel edge to obtain higher shear capacities, nailing requirements for structural members must be doubled, or alternate connectors, such as shear plates, must be used to maintain the load path.
(4) When wall sheathing is continuous over connected members, the tabulated number of nails can be reduced to 1-16d nail per foot.

Aluminum and Stainless-Steel Nails

Aluminum nails are sometimes used to fasten exterior siding. They're very resistant to rust and corrosion, but may corrode when used with some flashing metals.

Stainless steel. While expensive, stainless-steel nails are the most rust-resistant under nearly all conditions. They are highly recommended below grade or in homes that will be exposed to salt air. They're also recommended for cedar or redwood trim, and for siding that will be left to weather without stain or paint. Stainless-steel nails are typically available as Type 304 and 316. Type 316 are more durable.

Nailing Rules of Thumb

Typical nailing schedules appear in **Figure 16**.

Two is better than one. In general, never rely on a single nail. Use at least two.

Nail spacing. Don't space nails closer than one-quarter their length to the edge of the board.

Nail penetration. To hold at full strength, nails should penetrate the wood a depth that's at least 11 times their diameter — $1^{1/2}$ in. for 8d nails and $1^{3/4}$ in. for 16d nails.

Framing Connectors

Hangers for Solid Wood Joists

When using joist hangers, it's critical that you use the proper size hanger and fill all holes with nails.

Do not split ends. A nail that splits the wood will reduce the joist's carrying capacity. In critical situations, you can predrill nail holes a depth of up to three-quarters the nail's diameter.

Double-shear connectors provide greater strength with fewer nails (**Figure 17**).

Joist-Hanger Nails

A particular hanger may call for 8d, 10d, 12d, or 16d common nails. Special joist-hanger nails also may be used. Though they have 8d or 10d shank diameters, they are only $1^{1}/4$- to $1^{1}/2$-in. long, so they can be driven into the joist without protruding through the other side. Using them where the hanger calls for full-length 10d or 12d nails will reduce the hanger's load capacity by 20% to 30%. Hanger catalogs give adjustment factors for specific nail sizes. Don't use joist-hanger nails in place of longer nails

Figure 17. Double Shear Connectors

Double-shear connector

Double-shear nailing

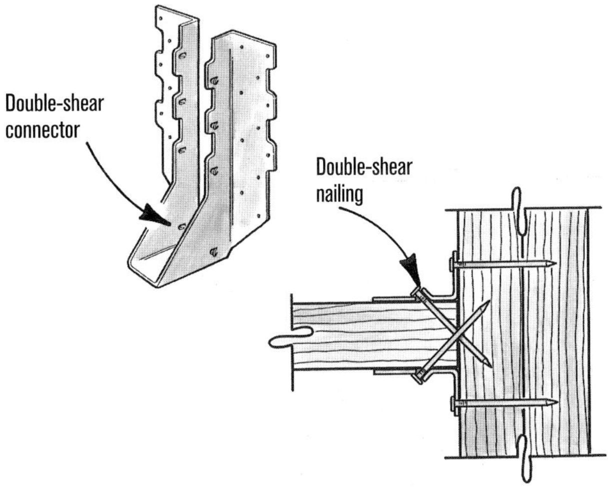

The strongest joist hangers are those that offer double shear nailing that crosses the joist ends. The angle also makes it easier to nail them to the joist in a joist bay.

in double-shear hangers or as face nails on skewed hangers.

Effect of Lumber Shrinkage on Hangers

Joist hangers are designed for use with dry lumber. If lumber is wet, shrinkage may leave a gap between the bottom of the joist and the hanger's saddle or between the top of the joist and the floor decking.

Figure 18. I-Joist Hanger Height

Figure 18. I-Joist Hanger Height

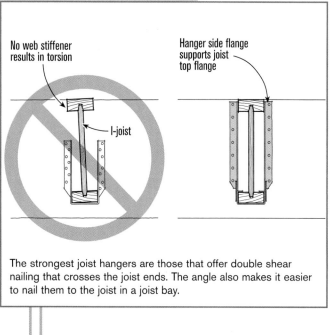

No web stiffener results in torsion

I-joist

Hanger side flange supports joist top flange

The strongest joist hangers are those that offer double shear nailing that crosses the joist ends. The angle also makes it easier to nail them to the joist in a joist bay.

Figure 19. Hangers on I-Joists

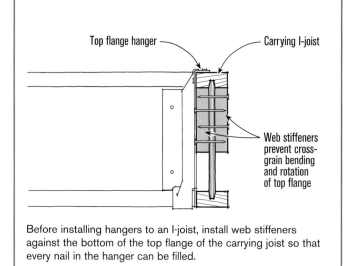

Top flange hanger

Carrying I-joist

Web stiffeners prevent cross-grain bending and rotation of top flange

Before installing hangers to an I-joist, install web stiffeners against the bottom of the top flange of the carrying joist so that every nail in the hanger can be filled.

Wood I-Joist Hangers

Wood I-joists require special hangers. Do not try to adapt conventional hangers.

I-Joist Hanger Height

Hangers for wood I-joists should be tall enough to catch the I-joist's top flange unless a web stiffener is used; otherwise, the joist may roll in the hanger (**Figure 18**). If a web stiffener is used, the hanger side flange should be at least 60% of the joist depth.

I-Joist Hanger Width

Hangers for wood I-joists should be the same width as the joist flange. Do not trim the flange to fit a narrower hanger; this would reduce the joist's strength. A wider hanger will either leave a gap, potentially causing a squeak, or will require filling with plywood, which would unevenly load the hanger.

Nailing I-Joist Hangers

Nail in every hole with correct sized nails; leaving nails out greatly reduces the hanger's capacity. Nails that are too long can hit the bottom of the hanger and curl under the joist, causing a squeak.

Web Stiffeners

For I-joist to I-joist connections, install web stiffeners against the bottom of the top flange of the carrying joist (**Figure 19**).

Wood Nailers for I-Joists

For hangers that bear on wood nailers, the nailer should not overhang its support more than $1/4$ in. or sit more than $1/8$ in. in from the edge (**Figure 20**).

Figure 20. I-Joist Hangers on Concrete and Steel

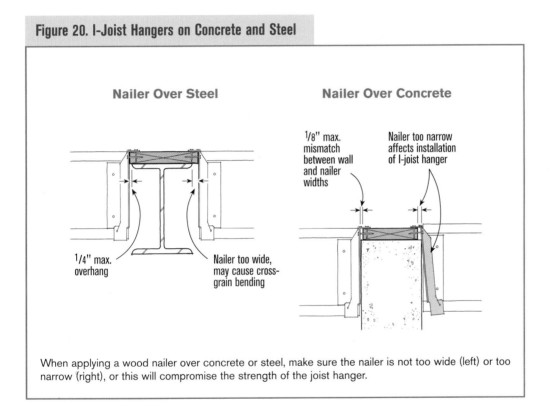

When applying a wood nailer over concrete or steel, make sure the nailer is not too wide (left) or too narrow (right), or this will compromise the strength of the joist hanger.

Floors: DIMENSIONAL LUMBER

Floor systems get their strength from the diaphragm action of the subflooring, which is typically T&G plywood glued and either nailed or screwed over uniformly spaced joists.

Joist Depth

Rule of thumb. Most codes assume residential floor loads to be 50 pounds per sq. ft. — 40 pounds live load plus 10 pounds dead load. If load conditions do not exceed this value, you can use the following rule of thumb for sizing uniformly loaded residential floor joists:

Figure 21. Live Loads for Floors and Ceilings

Component	Live Load (lbs./sq. ft.)
Residential rooms	40
Decks	60
Balconies	60
Fire escapes	40
Stairs	40
Ceiling joists (limited attic storage)	20
Ceiling joists (no attic storage)	10

Live loads include all loads that are not part of the building itself (dead loads), such as people, furnishings, wind, and snow.

HALF THE SPAN + 2 = JOIST DEPTH

First, round the clear span of the floor joist up to the nearest foot and divide by 2. Then add 2 to the answer. For example: For a clear span of 15 ft. 6 in., round up to 16 and divide this span by 2, giving you 8. Next, add 2 to get the required depth in inches ($8 + 2 = 10$). It's important to use the *actual* lumber dimensions, not the nominal dimensions, so a 2x12 floor joist will be required.

Design Loads for Floor Joists

Live loads. A 40-psf live load will meet most codes for residential living spaces (some require only 30 psf in bedrooms). For typical live loads, see **Figure 21**.

Dead loads. For dead loads, 10 psf is adequate for standard wood-frame construction. For mortar-set ceramic tile floors, frame for a 20-psf dead load. For other special situations, calculate loads based on weights of building materials (**Figure 22**).

Figure 22. Weights of Common Building Materials

Materials	Pounds per Sq. Ft.
Studs, Joists & Rafters	
2x4s, 16 in. o.c.	9
2x6s, 16 in. o.c.	1.4
2x6s, 24 in. o.c.	1
2x8s, 16 in. o.c.	1.9
2x8s, 24 in. o.c.	1.3
2x10s, 16 in. o.c.	2.4
2x10s, 24 in. o.c.	1.6
2x12s, 16 in. o.c.	2.9
2x12s, 24 in. o.c.	2
Residential roof truss, 24 in. o.c.	4
Sheet Goods	
$1/2$ in. plywood	1.5
$3/4$ in. plywood	2.3
$1/2$ in. drywall	2
$5/8$ in. drywall	2.5

This table can be used as an approximate guide for calculating dead loads. For the exact weight of specific materials, it's best to check with the manufacturer.

Materials	Pounds per Sq. Ft.
Flooring	
$3/4$ in. hardwood strip flooring	4
$3/8$ in. ceramic tile	2.5
$1/2$ in. quarry tile	6
1 in. mortar bed	12
Cement backerboard	3.5
Carpet and pad	3
Exterior Wall Cladding	
Wood siding	1.5
Three-coat stucco	10
Window unit	8
Roofing	
Asphalt shingles	2.5 - 4.5
Clay tiles	9 - 12
Spanish tile	19
Mortar bed for roof tile	10
Insulation (per in. thickness)	
Fiberglass batt insulation	.05
Rigid foam	.2

Joist Spacing

Floor and ceiling joists are usually framed 16 in. o.c. However they may be framed at 12 in. o.c. to increase stiffness, or to increase the span in one section of a floor system without changing lumber depth.

Joist Span Tables

Joist span means the clear, horizontal distance between supports (**Figure 23**). The actual joist length is longer to provide bearing at each end (see "I-Joist Bearing," page 31). Spans for dimensional lumber floor and ceiling joists are given in **Figures 24 to 27**, pages 94-97.

If the species or species group you are using is not listed, choose one with the same or slightly lower Fb values in **Figure 4**, page 6. If necessary, you can interpolate between two values.

Figure 23. Joist Span

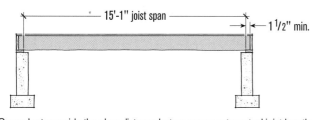

Span charts provide the clear distance between supports; actual joist length must include an additional bearing length on each end.

Figure 28. Anchor Bolt Placement

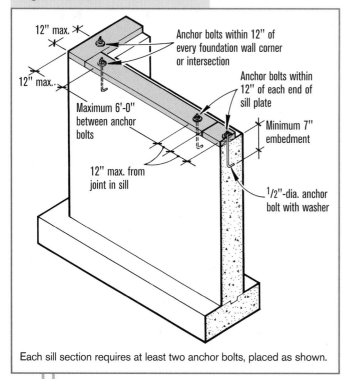

Each sill section requires at least two anchor bolts, placed as shown.

Framing Details

Sill Plates

For sill plates in contact with concrete or masonry foundations, use pressure-treated wood to protect against decay and insect attack.

Anchor Bolts

Bolt the sill plate to the foundation with anchor bolts or strap anchors spaced no more than 6 ft. apart.

Most codes call for minimum $1/2$-in. steel J-bolts embedded at least 7 in. in concrete, mortar joints, or solid-grouted masonry units. Each section of sill must have at least two bolts, with one bolt placed somewhere between $3^{1}/2$ to 12 in. from each end (**Figure 28**). Each bolt needs a nut and adequately sized washer.

Wedge anchors. If anchor bolts are missing, use $1/2$-in. wedge anchors or adhesive anchors that use hammer-in glass capsules. With a wedge anchor, tightening the nut expands the anchor until it's locked tight against the sides of the hole. A wedge anchor must be tightened to the manufacturer's specified torque. Tightening it too much can pulverize the surrounding concrete. Also, anchors can't be placed too close to the edge of a concrete slab or foundation wall.

Adhesive anchors. Adhesive anchors can be spaced closer to each other, and closer to the edge of a slab or wall, than wedge anchors. Drill a hole in the concrete and drop the capsule in. Then pound the anchor into the hole with a small sledgehammer; this mixes the chemicals in the capsule. Note: The capsules have a long shelf life, but should be protected from freezing.

Joist Bearing

Joists should have at least $1^1/2$ in. of good bearing on wood or metal, or 3 in. on masonry (**Figure 23**). If necessary, you can safely notch a joist at its bearing point up to one-sixth the depth of the joist.

Ceiling joists are often tapered to fit beneath the roof rafters. But tapering them too much will weaken the joists at their bearing point. If you must taper the ends of a ceiling joist, follow the guideline shown in **Figure 29**.

Boring and Notching Joists

In general, do not make any notches in the middle third of a joist. Also, avoid vertical cuts in the bottom of a joist; angle the cuts instead to reduce the likelihood of splitting. For other rules, follow the recommendations in **Figure 30**.

Figure 29. Tapered Joist Ends

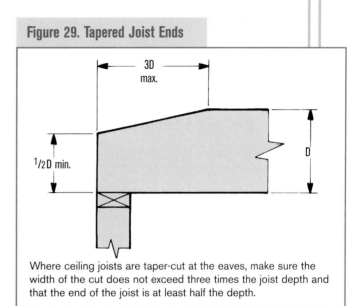

Where ceiling joists are taper-cut at the eaves, make sure the width of the cut does not exceed three times the joist depth and that the end of the joist is at least half the depth.

Figure 30. Cutting, Notching, and Boring Lumber Joists

Joist Size	Maximum Hole	Maximum Notch Depth	Maximum End Notch
2x4	None	None	None
2x6	$1^1/2$	$^7/8$	$1^3/8$
2x8	$2^3/8$	$1^1/4$	$1^7/8$
2x10	3	$1^1/2$	$2^3/8$
2x12	$3^3/4$	$1^7/8$	$2^7/8$

Do not notch a span's middle third where bending forces are greatest. For all calculations, use actual, not nominal, dimensions.

Where mechanicals need to pass through a joist supporting a partition, double the joist with blocking in between to create a cavity (**Figure 31**).

Rim Joists and Bridging

To prevent joists from twisting, the ends must be nailed to a solid band joist (rim joist) or header. If there is no band joist or header, nail solid blocking between the joist ends. Most codes don't require additional bridging unless the joist is at least six times as high as it is wide, in which case bridging is needed every 8 ft. However, solid or X-type bridging at mid-span will help stiffen any floor.

Load Paths

All loads start at the roof and must transfer on an unbroken path through structural elements to the foundation. Many cracking problems, which are misinterpreted as "settling," are actually caused by broken load paths. These broken paths result in loads being carried by areas that were not designed to carry them.

Support for Loadbearing Walls

Parallel to joists. Ideally, if a loadbearing wall runs parallel to the floor joists, then it should sit directly over a beam or a joist supported by a loadbearing wall below. If the loadbearing wall sits between two joists, complete the load path by installing solid blocking between the two joists every 16 in. o.c.

Perpendicular to joists. If a loadbearing wall runs perpendicular to the floor joists, it should be offset from a supporting beam or loadbearing wall below by no more than the depth of the joists (**Figure 32**).

Figure 31. Accommodating Mechanicals

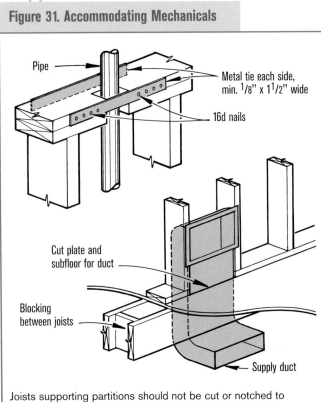

Pipe

Metal tie each side, min. $1/8$" x $1^1/2$" wide

16d nails

Cut plate and subfloor for duct

Blocking between joists

Supply duct

Joists supporting partitions should not be cut or notched to accommodate mechanicals. Instead, double the joist with blocking in between to create a cavity.

Support for Non-Loadbearing Walls

A non-loadbearing wall that runs parallel to the joists doesn't need to be placed directly over a joist. However, when it's not directly over a joist, solid blocking should be installed between the joists to carry the load (**Figure 33**). If the wall is placed directly over a joist, that joist should be doubled.

Point Loads

A concentrated load that bears on a floor system — such as a structural post — must sit directly over a post or beam below. In addition, solid blocking (with a cross-section at least as large as the post) must carry the load through the floor system to the underlying post or beam.

Figure 32. Aligning Bearing Walls

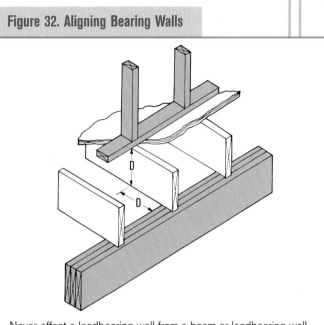

Never offset a loadbearing wall from a beam or loadbearing wall below by more than the depth of the joists.

Figure 33. Blocking under Non-Loadbearing Walls

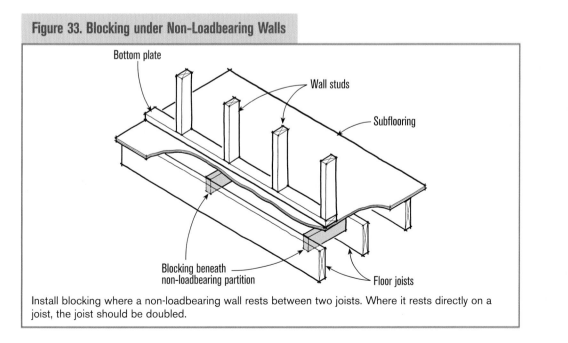

Install blocking where a non-loadbearing wall rests between two joists. Where it rests directly on a joist, the joist should be doubled.

Floor Openings

Where a floor opening is more than 4 ft. wide, both the headers and trimmers should be doubled (**Figure 34**). Headers over 6 ft. long must be fastened with steel connectors and should be sized according to the load.

A tail joist in a framed opening that's over 12 ft. long should be connected with hangers. Otherwise, it should sit on a 2x2 (min.) ledger nailed to the face of the header.

Figure 34. Framed Openings

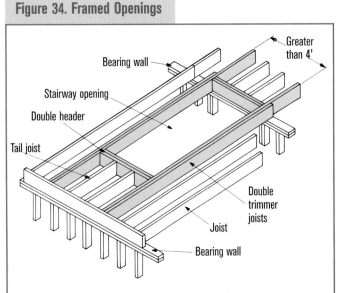

Where a header in a floor opening exceeds 4 ft., double the headers and trimmers. Where the header exceeds 6 ft., it should be installed with framing anchors.

Cantilevered Floors

Basic framing details for all cantilevers are shown in **Figure 35**.

Loadbearing Cantilevers

Where a cantilevered floor supports only a roof load with a total span of 28 ft. or less (such as on a Garrison-style home), the joists may cantilever up to one-eighth the length of the lumber span. Where the loads are greater, the cantilever should not exceed the depth of the joists unless the system is engineered.

Non-Loadbearing Cantilevers

A cantilever that supports a non-load-bearing wall should not exceed one-fourth the joist span. For non-load-bearing cantilevered decks (floor load only), the maximum overhang is one-third the span (**Figure 36**).

Engineered Cantilevers

Cantilevers that exceed these limits should be engineered. Doubling joists or reducing joist spaces, along with upgrading connections, often permits greater overhangs.

Figure 35. Cantilever Details

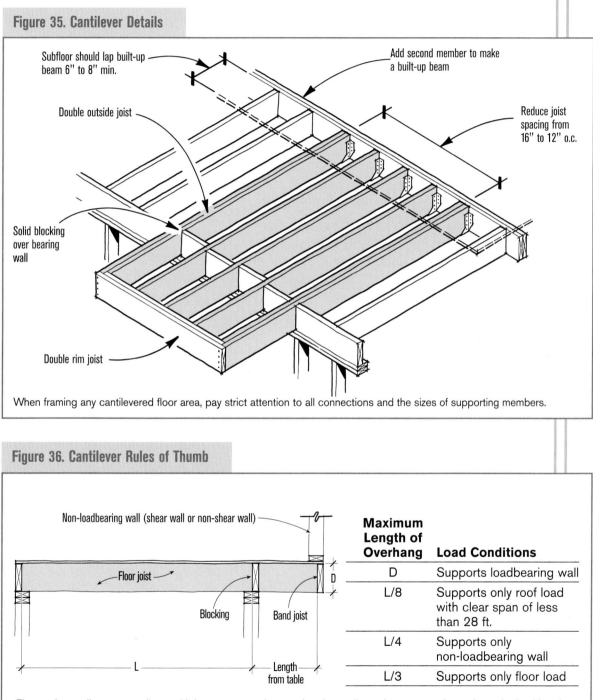

Subfloor should lap built-up beam 6" to 8" min.

Add second member to make a built-up beam

Double outside joist

Reduce joist spacing from 16" to 12" o.c.

Solid blocking over bearing wall

Double rim joist

When framing any cantilevered floor area, pay strict attention to all connections and the sizes of supporting members.

Figure 36. Cantilever Rules of Thumb

Non-loadbearing wall (shear wall or non-shear wall)

Floor joist

Blocking

Band joist

D

L

Length from table

Maximum Length of Overhang	Load Conditions
D	Supports loadbearing wall
L/8	Supports only roof load with clear span of less than 28 ft.
L/4	Supports only non-loadbearing wall
L/3	Supports only floor load

The maximum distance cantilevered joists may extend past a bearing wall or other support depends on the load bearing on the end of the cantilever.

Floors: SUBFLOORING

The best quality subfloor consists of tongue-and-groove (T&G) plywood that's glued and either nailed or screwed to the joists. T&G subflooring improves the perceived stiffness of the floor, and helps prevent squeaks. Subflooring that is not T&G must have solid blocking under all joints between panels.

Subfloor Spans

While T&G subflooring does not require solid blocking at joints, every sheet must rest on at least two joists. Panels are rated for spans of 16-, 20-, or 24-in., depending on thickness and grade. Span information is stamped on individual sheets (**Figure 8**, page 9).

Fastening Subfloor Panels

Nail panels with minimum 6d common nails, spaced 6 in. o.c. at the edges of the panel and 12 in. o.c. in the field. Keep nails at least $3/8$ in. from edges. (For shear wall nailing requirements, see "Shear Walls," page 74.)

For nailing schedules, see **Figure 16**, pages 16-17.

Gaps for Subfloor

APA recommends that subfloor panels be gapped $1/8$ in. along the ends and edges. A 10d box nail may be used to gauge the spacing.

Gluing Subfloor

When nailing subfloor panels to joists under wet conditions, use a construction adhesive labeled AFG-01 and/or ASTM D 3498. Solvent-based construction adhesives typically dissipate the water better than latex- and urethane-based adhesives.

Roof and Wall Sheathing

Do not glue roof or wall sheathing to framing. Sheathing panels tend to be thinner than subflooring panels, so they're more likely to buckle when wet.

Floors: WOOD I-JOISTS

Spans, installation details, and other wood I-joist specifications vary from one manufacturer to the next. Therefore, it is important to consult the manufacturer's literature when using these products.

Boring and Notching I-Joists

Rules vary, depending on the I-joist manufacturer, but the following guidelines generally apply to cutting holes in wood I-joists.

No Holes Through Flanges

Never make holes or saw cuts in I-joist flanges — the bending stresses are too high. Even a shallow kerf in the lower flange can critically weaken an I-joist.

Holes in Webs

Follow manufacturers' guidelines for minimum distances between holes and the bearing point (**Figure 37**). Use manufacturers' knockouts where practical. In general, you can cut a hole up to $1^1/2$ in. in diameter anywhere in the web.

Hole size. Permissible hole size increases as you near the center of the span where shear stresses are the smallest. Most manufacturers require that the distance between two holes be at least twice the diameter of the larger hole.

Avoid rectangular cutouts. With rectangular holes in webs, avoid overcutting the corners. Rounded corners are best. One technique is to drill a 1-in. hole in each corner and then cut between the holes.

I-Joist Bearing

Most I-joists require at least $1^3/4$ in. of bearing at each end. If the end of the joist is cut at a bevel, the top chord must also extend beyond the face of the wall (**Figure 38**).

Temporary Bracing for I-Joists

Unbraced I-joists are flimsy and unstable until they are fully braced and sheathed. It doesn't take much to roll them over and damage them, so install

Figure 37. Cutting and Notching Rules for Wood I-Joists

I-Joist Depth	TJI/Pro	Hole Diameter				
9$\frac{1}{2}$"	150	1'-0"	1'-6"	3'-0"	5'-0"	6'-6"
	250	1'-0"	2'-6"	4'-0"	5'-6"	7'-6"
11$\frac{7}{8}$"	150	1'-0"	1'-0"	1'-0"	2'-0"	3'-0"
	250	1'-0"	1'-0"	2'-0"	3'-0"	4'-6"
	350	1'-0"	2'-0"	3'-0"	4'-6"	5'-6"
	550	1'-0"	1'-6"	3'-0"	4'-6"	6'-0"
14"	250	1'-0"	1'-0"	1'-0"	1'-0"	1'-6"
	350	1'-0"	1'-0"	1'-0"	1'-6"	3'-0"
	550	1'-0"	1'-0"	1'-0"	2'-6"	4'-0"
16"	250	1'-0"	1'-0"	1'-0"	1'-0"	1'-0"
	350	1'-0"	1'-0"	1'-0"	1'-0"	1'-0"
	550	1'-0"	1'-0"	1'-0"	1'-0"	2'-0"

Min. Distance (ft.-in.) from Inside Face of Support to Near Edge of Hole

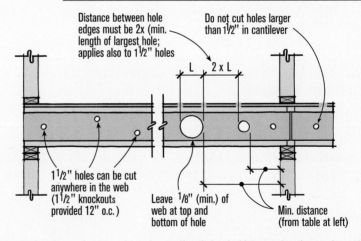

Distance between hole edges must be 2x (min. length of largest hole; applies also to 1½" holes

Do not cut holes larger than 1½" in cantilever

L   2 x L

1½" holes can be cut anywhere in the web (1½" knockouts provided 12" o.c.)

Leave ⅛" (min.) of web at top and bottom of hole

Min. distance (from table at left)

Note: Distances in the charts above are based on uniformly loaded joists using the maximum loads shown in Trus Joist's brochure. For other load conditions or hole configurations, contact a Trus Joist representative. For simple span (5-foot minimum) uniformly loaded joists, one maximum-size hole may be located at the center of the joist span provided no other holes occur in the joist. DO NOT cut into joist flanges when cutting out web.

Most manufacturers allow holes up to 1½ in. anywhere in the web, but require that the distance between any two holes be at least twice the diameter of the larger hole. In all cases, follow manufacturer's specifications for hole locations. The example provided here is courtesy of Trus Joist. Larger holes are allowed per manufacturer's specification.

all blocking and rim boards as soon as possible.

Sheathing and 1x4 Bracing

Stabilize the joists by sheathing the first 4 ft. of the floor system at one end of the joist bays and then bracing the rest of the joists to the sheathing area with 1x4 braces placed every 6 to 8 ft. Nail the braces flat to the top of the joists and lap them at the ends by at least two joists.

Avoid Overloading I-Joists

Be careful not to overload I-joists with heavy construction materials, such as stacks of plywood or pallets of bricks. If such loads are unavoidable, place them directly over loadbearing walls, posts, or other suitable supports.

I-Joist Load Paths

Loadbearing walls should be stacked over girders or loadbearing walls below. Use squash blocks or I-joist blocking to carry the load through the floor system (**Figure 39**).

Do not offset loadbearing walls unless the design has been engineered.

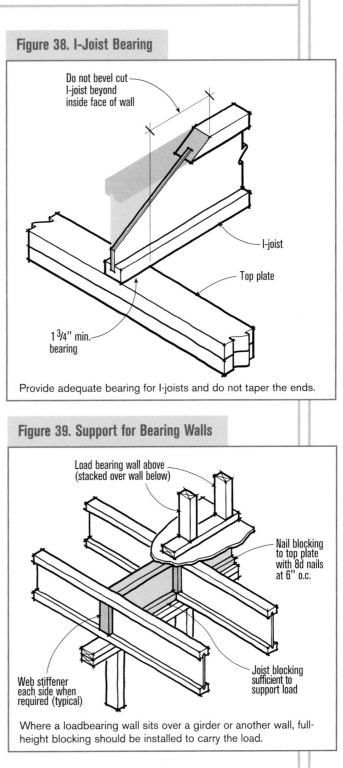

Figure 38. I-Joist Bearing

Do not bevel cut I-joist beyond inside face of wall

I-joist

Top plate

1 3/4" min. bearing

Provide adequate bearing for I-joists and do not taper the ends.

Figure 39. Support for Bearing Walls

Load bearing wall above (stacked over wall below)

Nail blocking to top plate with 8d nails at 6" o.c.

Web stiffener each side when required (typical)

Joist blocking sufficient to support load

Where a loadbearing wall sits over a girder or another wall, full-height blocking should be installed to carry the load.

Figure 40. Rim Joists

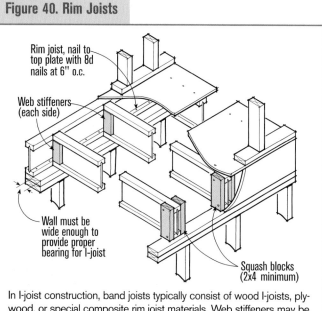

Rim joist, nail to top plate with 8d nails at 6" o.c.

Web stiffeners (each side)

Wall must be wide enough to provide proper bearing for I-joist

Squash blocks (2x4 minimum)

In I-joist construction, band joists typically consist of wood I-joists, plywood, or special composite rim joist materials. Web stiffeners may be required on long spans. Squash blocks may be required with thinner rim joist materials when there is a loadbearing wall above. Check manufacturer's specifications.

Figure 41. Web Stiffeners

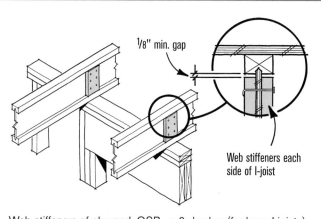

1/8" min. gap

Web stiffeners each side of I-joist

Web stiffeners of plywood, OSB, or 2x lumber (for large I-joists) are required at certain bearing points to transfer shear and prevent buckling of the web. Except where there is a concentrated load from above, web stiffeners should fit tight to the bottom flange with a space at the top. Web stiffeners also provide solid nailing at joist hangers. Follow manufacturers' nailing schedules.

Rim Joists for I-Joist Floors

To keep joists from twisting — and to help transfer loads from the wall above to the wall or foundation below — either attach the ends of I-joists to a full-height (band) joist or header or install blocking between the joists.

Rim Joist Materials

Acceptable rim joist materials include: the same-size I-joists as those used in the floor system; one or two layers of plywood or OSB; or an engineered lumber or metal product (**Figure 40**).

Don't mix wood I-joists with solid lumber rim joists. Not only are the two materials difficult to match in height, but also solid lumber will shrink after installation, leaving too much weight on the I-joists.

Web Stiffeners for I-Joists

Web stiffeners of plywood, OSB, or 2x are used to keep I-joist webs from buckling at bearing points or other intersections. (Thin web materials cannot transfer large shear forces.) With joist hangers, web stiffeners are often required to provide solid nailing.

Web stiffeners at bearing points should be installed tight to the top of the bottom flange. Leave a 1/8- to 1/4-in. space at the top flange to prevent the stiffener from prying the top flange off under load (**Figure 41**). One exception is where the joists support a load from above at mid-span. In this case, install the stiffener tight to the top flange with the space at the bottom.

Web stiffeners go on both sides of an I-joist with the face grain parallel to the length of the joist (for plywood and OSB stiffeners). Nail plywood or OSB stiffeners from each side with three or more 8d nails, staggered and clinched at the ends. For solid 2x stiffeners, use three 16d nails (two from one side, one from the other) and clinch the ends if they penetrate. In all cases, follow manufacturers' nailing schedules.

Squash Blocks for I-Joists

Squash blocks are required under concentrated loads such as posts and, in some cases, where the joists must transfer the load from a bearing wall above to another bearing wall below.

Squash blocks should be slightly larger than the depth of the joists to ensure that they pick up the full load. Fasten blocks to the top and bottom joist flanges with 8d nails (**Figure 42**).

Filler Blocks for I-Joists

Where two or more I-joists serve as a girder, the web area should be filled in with solid blocking of plywood, OSB, or dimensional lumber. The filler will ensure that both members carry the load.

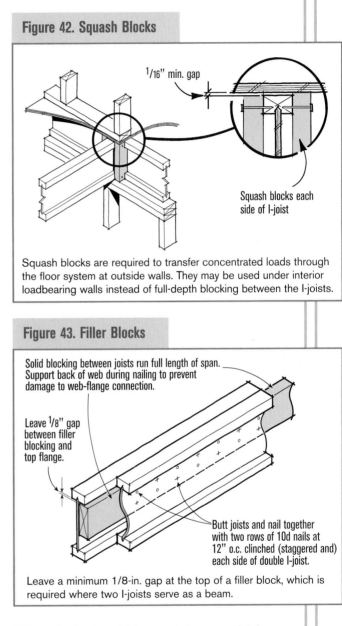

Figure 42. Squash Blocks

1/16" min. gap

Squash blocks each side of I-joist

Squash blocks are required to transfer concentrated loads through the floor system at outside walls. They may be used under interior loadbearing walls instead of full-depth blocking between the I-joists.

Figure 43. Filler Blocks

Solid blocking between joists run full length of span. Support back of web during nailing to prevent damage to web-flange connection.

Leave 1/8" gap between filler blocking and top flange.

Butt joists and nail together with two rows of 10d nails at 12" o.c. clinched (staggered and) each side of double I-joist.

Leave a minimum 1/8-in. gap at the top of a filler block, which is required where two I-joists serve as a beam.

Filler pieces should be a minimum of 4 ft. long, depending on the manufacturers' specs, and should be installed with a gap at the top (**Figure 43**). Nails should be clinched to prevent pullout.

Figure 44. Backer Blocks

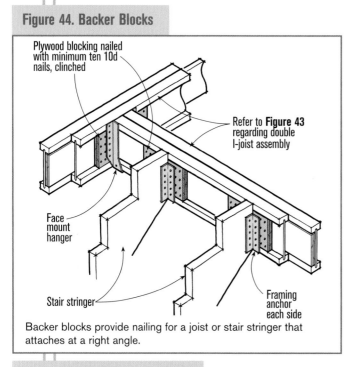

Plywood blocking nailed with minimum ten 10d nails, clinched

Refer to **Figure 43** regarding double I-joist assembly

Face mount hanger

Stair stringer

Framing anchor each side

Backer blocks provide nailing for a joist or stair stringer that attaches at a right angle.

Figure 45. Cantilevered I-Joists

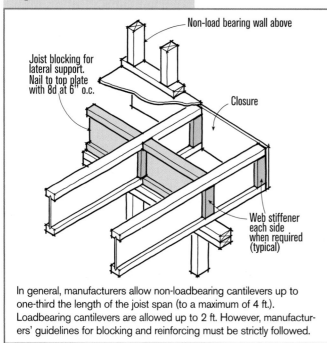

Non-load bearing wall above

Joist blocking for lateral support. Nail to top plate with 8d at 6" o.c.

Closure

Web stiffener each side when required (typical)

In general, manufacturers allow non-loadbearing cantilevers up to one-third the length of the joist span (to a maximum of 4 ft.). Loadbearing cantilevers are allowed up to 2 ft. However, manufacturers' guidelines for blocking and reinforcing must be strictly followed.

Floor Openings

Where a joist or stair stringer attaches to the side of an I-joist, nail backer blocks to the web to provide a nailing surface. These full-width blocks should extend 6 to 12 in. past either side of the intersecting joist or stringer and may be needed on both sides of the web (**Figure 44**). Refer to the manufacturer's literature for details.

Cantilevered I-Joists

There are several ways to frame cantilevers with I-joists. Most manufacturers permit non-loadbearing cantilevers up to one-third the length of the joist span (to a maximum of 4 ft.). Loadbearing cantilevers may be up to 2 ft. long. Since a cantilever can easily over-stress an I-joist that's not reinforced, it's important to strictly follow the manufacturer's guidelines for allowable spans and required blocking. **Figure 45** shows some sample details.

Floors: TRUSSES

Structurally, an open-web floor truss resembles an I-beam in that it puts most of its material along its top and bottom edges where stresses are greatest. To strengthen a truss, the fabricator may double its top and bottom chords, make side-by-side girder trusses, use larger truss plates or stronger wood, or use some combination of these techniques.

Truss Types

Floor trusses can be designed to sit on either their bottom chord or their top chord (**Figure 46**).

Handling Trusses

When receiving a truckload of trusses, reject those with excessive splits in chords or braces, those with knots close to metal plates, or those with loose or deformed plates. Also reject any that show evidence of having been damaged and repaired. Beware of warped or wet lumber, which can set up dangerous stresses as it shrinks and dries.

Figure 46. Truss Types

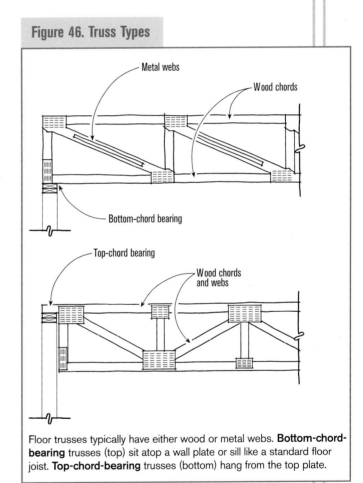

Floor trusses typically have either wood or metal webs. **Bottom-chord-bearing** trusses (top) sit atop a wall plate or sill like a standard floor joist. **Top-chord-bearing** trusses (bottom) hang from the top plate.

Caution: Loose Plates

Connector plates should be centered over the joint and firmly embedded in the wood. Never refasten a loose plate: The bond cannot be restored once it's been broken.

Lifting With a Crane

If you use a crane, always lift from two points (**Figure 47**) and never lift the truss sideways; the excess flexing can loosen the connector plates, causing eventual failure.

Installing Floor Trusses

Floor trusses are usually spaced 24 in. o.c., and are typically lifted by hand, rolled into place, fastened, and braced.

Right Side Up

It is crucial to install each truss right side up, according to the label attached to the truss. Each web member is designed to be in compression or tension, but not both.

Bearing at Center Girder

A bottom-chord-bearing truss that crosses a girder or bearing wall may be designed to function as two simple beams. In this case, a tag attached to the truss will indicate that the top chord should be cut after installation (**Figure 48**). Without this cut, a load

Figure 47. Lifting Floor Trusses by Crane

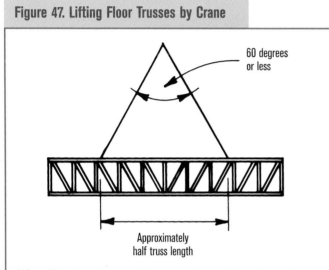

60 degrees or less

Approximately half truss length

When lifting floor trusses with a crane, always lift from two points and never lift the truss sideways, which can loosen connector plates.

Figure 48. Special Field Cuts

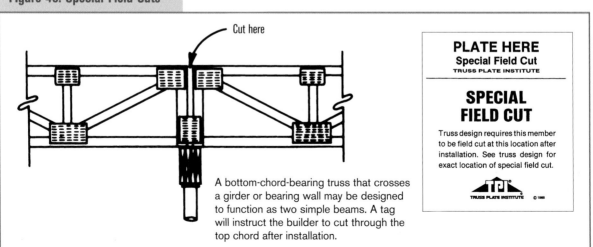

Cut here

A bottom-chord-bearing truss that crosses a girder or bearing wall may be designed to function as two simple beams. A tag will instruct the builder to cut through the top chord after installation.

PLATE HERE
Special Field Cut
TRUSS PLATE INSTITUTE

SPECIAL FIELD CUT

Truss design requires this member to be field cut at this location after installation. See truss design for exact location of special field cut.

TRUSS PLATE INSTITUTE © 1988

Figure 49. Stairwell Openings

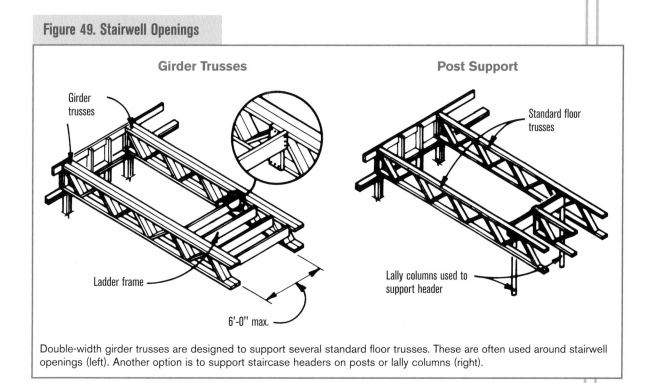

Girder Trusses

Girder trusses

Ladder frame

6'-0" max.

Post Support

Standard floor trusses

Lally columns used to support header

Double-width girder trusses are designed to support several standard floor trusses. These are often used around stairwell openings (left). Another option is to support staircase headers on posts or lally columns (right).

applied to one end of the truss will lift the other, creating a seesaw action.

Stairwell Openings

Girder trusses are designed to support several standard floor trusses. These are often used around stairwell openings (**Figure 49**).

Bracing Floor Trusses

Bracing prevents trusses from bending, twisting, or otherwise deforming. On bottom-chord-bearing trusses, the ends are tied together with 2x4 ledgers

that also serve as a nailing base for the perimeter of the plywood deck (**Figure 50**). Underneath, 2x6 strongbacks laid on edge should run continuously through the webs of all the trusses at 10-ft. intervals (one run for a 20-ft. truss, two runs for longer trusses). The 2x6 serves the same purpose as bridging in a standard floor, distributing concentrated loads over a wider area.

Fire-Stopping for Floor Trusses

Top-chord-bearing trusses short-circuit the fire-stopping ordinarily provided by the top plate. Common solutions are to extend the drywall past the trusses to the top plate, or to insert a separate 2x4 fire stop inside each stud bay just below the bottom chord of the truss (**Figure 51**). Check with local codes for requirements in your area.

Figure 50. Bracing Bottom-Chord-Bearing Trusses

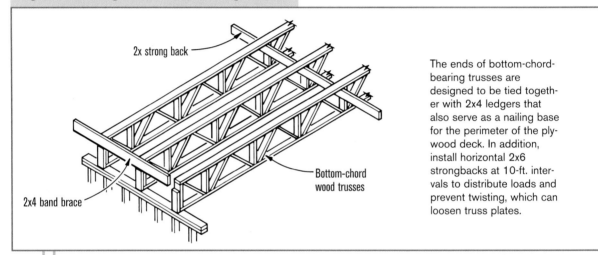

2x strong back

Bottom-chord wood trusses

2x4 band brace

The ends of bottom-chord-bearing trusses are designed to be tied together with 2x4 ledgers that also serve as a nailing base for the perimeter of the plywood deck. In addition, install horizontal 2x6 strongbacks at 10-ft. intervals to distribute loads and prevent twisting, which can loosen truss plates.

Figure 51. Fire-Stopping for Open-Web Trusses

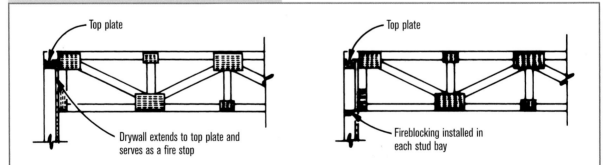

Top plate

Top plate

Drywall extends to top plate and serves as a fire stop

Fireblocking installed in each stud bay

Many codes require fire-stopping with open-web trusses at the intersections of wall and ceiling spaces. Techniques include extending the drywall past the truss to the top plate (left), or installing a 2x4 fire-stop inside each stud bay just below the truss's bottom chord (right).

Walls

Stud Spacing

Maximum stud spacing for Standard or better-grade studs is shown in **Figure 52**. Lower-grade 2x4 studs cannot exceed 16 in. o.c.

Top Plates

Most model codes require loadbearing walls to have double top plates lapped so that the splices are at least 4 ft. apart. Two 16d nails are required on each side of the splice and additional nails are required every 24 in. in the overlap area (**Figure 53**). See nailing schedules (**Figure 16**, pages 16-17) for air-nail requirements.

Double vs. Single Top Plates

Single top plates are considerably weaker than a traditional double top plate. However, many codes permit single top plates as long as they are joined at splices, corners, and intersecting walls with .036-in.-thick galvanized steel plates, measuring 3x6 in. Plates should be fastened with six 8d nails on each side (six nails for ICBO).

Figure 52. Maximum Stud Spacing (in.)

Stud Size	Supporting Roof and Ceiling Only	Supporting One Floor Roof and Ceiling	Supporting Two Floors Roof and Ceiling
2x4	24*	16	–
2x6	24	24	16

* Shall be reduced to 16 inches if Utility grade studs are used.
Adapted from IRC Table R-602.3(5)

Figure 53. Splicing Top Plates in Bearing Walls

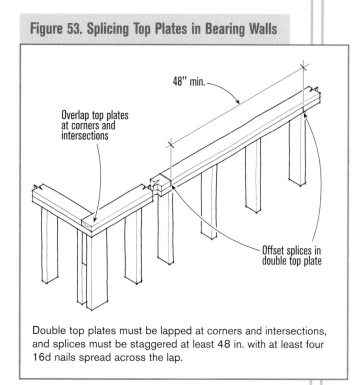

Overlap top plates at corners and intersections

48" min.

Offset splices in double top plate

Double top plates must be lapped at corners and intersections, and splices must be staggered at least 48 in. with at least four 16d nails spread across the lap.

Figure 54. Double vs. Single Top Plate

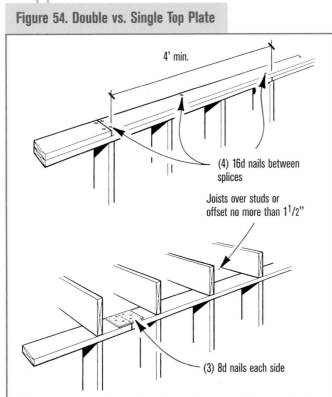

4' min.

(4) 16d nails between splices

Joists over studs or offset no more than 1^1/$_2$"

(3) 8d nails each side

Although some model codes allow a single top plate with steel connectors and joists lined up over studs, the traditional double top plate produces a stronger wall.

Figure 55. Notching and Boring Regular Studs

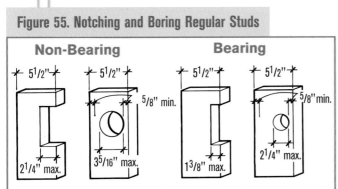

Non-Bearing

5^1/$_2$"   5^1/$_2$"   5/8" min.   2^1/$_4$" max.   3^5/$_{16}$" max.

Bearing

5^1/$_2$"   5^1/$_2$"   5/8" min.   1^3/$_8$" max.   2^1/$_4$" max.

Notches in loadbearing studs under 10-ft.-tall should not exceed 25% of the stud depth and should not occur in the middle third of the stud. Bored holes should not exceed 40% of the stud depth and should be at least 5/8 in. from the edge. See **Figure 9,** page 11 for notching and drilling studs over 10 ft. tall.

When using single top plates, rafters or joists must not be offset from studs by more than 1^1/$_2$ in. (**Figure 54**).

Maximum Stud Lengths

Studs used in exterior loadbearing walls, whether 2x4 or 2x6, should not be more than 10 ft. high without being engineered.

Engineered solutions include reducing stud spacing, using wider studs, doubling the studs, and using studs made from engineered lumber.

Notching and Boring Studs and Plates

Studs

When notching or drilling through studs under 10 ft. tall, follow the guidelines shown in **Figure 55**. Never make notches and holes across from one another in the same section of a stud. For studs over 10 ft. in height, follow guidelines shown in **Figure 9**, page 11.

Plates

If more than 50% of the width of a top plate is notched or drilled away, then the edge of the plate must be reinforced with a 24-gauge steel plate that spans the distance between the adjoining studs (**Figure 31**, page 26).

Corner Studs

On three-stud corners, builders often replace the middle stud with wood spacers. While that is acceptable in most cases, the three-stud corner is more than just a nailer for sheathing or drywall — it must also transfer shear loads between adjoining walls (**Figure 56**). For this reason, don't omit the third stud where shear resistance is critical.

Wall Bracing

In most residential construction, plywood or OSB sheathing panels are used for lateral bracing and are nailed 6 in. o.c. at the edges and 12 in. o.c. in the field. This provides excellent racking resistance. Bracing values for plywood can be improved by using larger nails or by spacing nails more closely together.

Bracing with Foam Sheathing

When using a non-structural sheathing such as foam board, install bracing at the building corners to provide resistance to racking. This bracing may consist of diagonal 1x4s or vertical sheets of plywood or OSB (**Figure 57**).

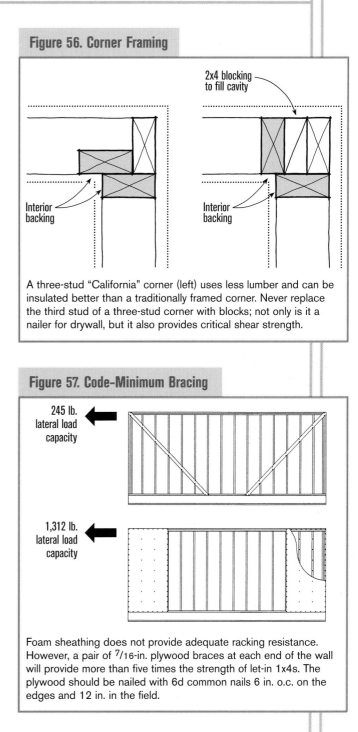

Figure 56. Corner Framing

2x4 blocking to fill cavity

Interior backing

Interior backing

A three-stud "California" corner (left) uses less lumber and can be insulated better than a traditionally framed corner. Never replace the third stud of a three-stud corner with blocks; not only is it a nailer for drywall, but it also provides critical shear strength.

Figure 57. Code-Minimum Bracing

245 lb. lateral load capacity

1,312 lb. lateral load capacity

Foam sheathing does not provide adequate racking resistance. However, a pair of $7/16$-in. plywood braces at each end of the wall will provide more than five times the strength of let-in 1x4s. The plywood should be nailed with 6d common nails 6 in. o.c. on the edges and 12 in. in the field.

Figure 58. Header Options

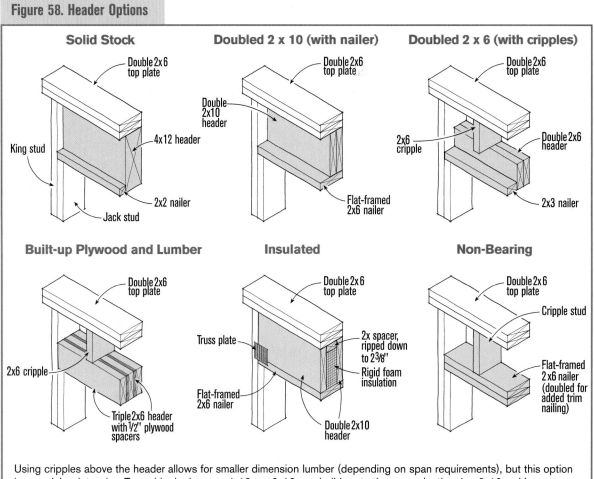

Using cripples above the header allows for smaller dimension lumber (depending on span requirements), but this option is more labor intensive. To avoid cripples, use 4x12s or 2x12s, or build up to the same depth using 2x10s with an added flat-framed member.

Diagonal bracing. Diagonal bracing is typically notched into the top and bottom plates and all intervening studs, and nailed with two 8d nails at each stud. Use ¾-in. plywood instead of 1x4s for braces.

Metal Bracing

Depending on code, T-shaped metal bracing may sometimes be used in place of wood bracing — typically only as temporary bracing during construction.

Wind Bracing

In earthquake-prone or high-wind areas, pay special attention to the nailing of wall and roof sheathing, as well as to all the vertical framing connections that structurally join the building from foundation to roof. Consult local codes for nailing requirements (see also "Shear Walls," page 74).

Headers

Window and door headers can be framed in a variety of ways, depending on the lumber available and the insulation requirements, as shown in **Figure 58**.

Header Height

Set headers at the height of door rough openings. For a standard pre-hung door, the header height needs to be at least 6 ft. 10 in. (**Figure 59**).

Set window headers at the same height as doors so all openings align.

Rim-joist headers. In a two-story house, rough opening heights can be raised by doubling up on the rim joist, or creating a girder to meet structural requirements for the span (see span tables, pages 98-103).

Sizing Headers

Rough openings in loadbearing walls require headers that are supported at either end by jack studs (trimmers). Header sizes for various house configurations and the number of jack studs required at each end are shown in **Figures 60 through 65**, pages 98-103.

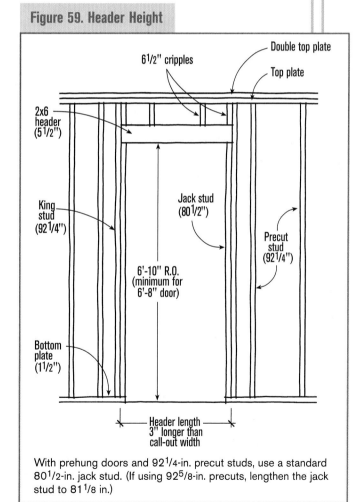

Figure 59. Header Height

6 1/2" cripples

Double top plate

Top plate

2x6 header (5 1/2")

King stud (92 1/4")

Jack stud (80 1/2")

Precut stud (92 1/4")

6'-10" R.O. (minimum for 6'-8" door)

Bottom plate (1 1/2")

Header length 3" longer than call-out width

With prehung doors and 92 1/4-in. precut studs, use a standard 80 1/2-in. jack stud. (If using 92 5/8-in. precuts, lengthen the jack stud to 81 1/8 in.)

Figure 66. Cantilevered Headers

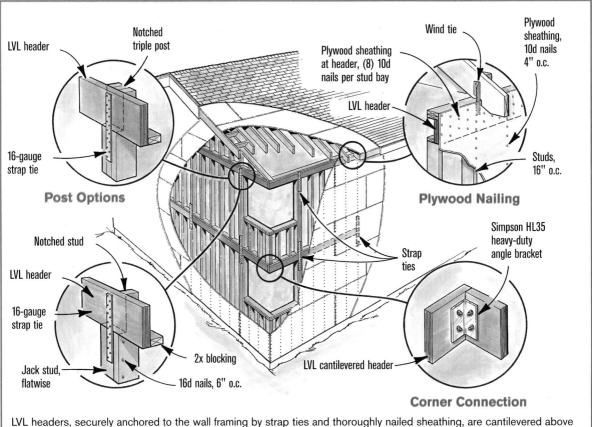

LVL headers, securely anchored to the wall framing by strap ties and thoroughly nailed sheathing, are cantilevered above the window opening. For a two-story structure, the lower header may be built-in as the rim joist.

Corner Window Headers

A corner window requires a cantilevered header. **Figure 66** shows the basic building details for such cantilevered headers. To meet actual load conditions, an engineer should specify header dimensions and connection criteria.

Even with proper header sizing, some deflection may occur. Do not nail the window directly to the header. Manufacturers of corner windows provide metal installation clips to isolate the windows from the rough opening. These clips should be installed using foam backer rod between the header jam and the rough opening. Secure trim to the jamb with a minimal number of light-gauge nails.

Fire-Stopping Details for Walls

In general, residential building codes call for fire stops at the following locations (**Figure 67**):

- In stud walls and partitions at every floor and ceiling level, including furred spaces;

- At every 10 ft. of vertical distance in tall walls or partitions;

- At all interconnections between vertical and horizontal concealed spaces, such as at soffits, cove ceilings, and drop ceilings;

- In the stud spaces along the side of stair stringers;

- At openings around pipes, ducts, chimneys, and fireplaces at floor and ceiling levels.

Fire-Stop Materials

Code-approved fire-stop materials include nominal 2-in.-thick lumber, double layers of 3/4-in. plywood or particleboard (with joints backed by the same material), 1/2-in.-thick drywall, and 1/2-in. cement board. Unfaced fiberglass batts can be used as fire-stopping under IRC R602.8.1.1 as long the batts fill the stud cavity for at least 16 in. of vertical space.

Irregular Openings

All fire stops should be cut to fit tightly. Voids of more than 1/8 in. will undermine the material's fire-stopping ability. For irregularly shaped openings, use an "intumescent" fire-stopping compound. Because these products expand when heated, they will fill the void left by plastic piping or cable insulation that has melted away.

Figure 67. Fire-Stop Details

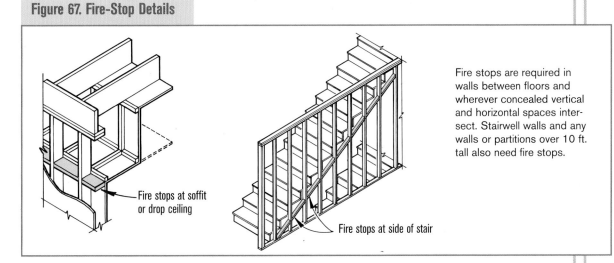

Fire stops at soffit or drop ceiling

Fire stops at side of stair

Fire stops are required in walls between floors and wherever concealed vertical and horizontal spaces intersect. Stairwell walls and any walls or partitions over 10 ft. tall also need fire stops.

Roofs: DIMENSIONAL LUMBER

Rafter Loads

Loads on residential rafters typically include snow and wind (the most common live loads), roofing materials, and interior finish materials (dead loads).

Live loading conditions for roofs vary widely with snow and wind loads. Be sure to check local codes for structural design requirements in your area.

For precise dead load calculations, refer to the material weights shown in **Figure 22**, page 23.

Common Rafter Spans

Rafter span is the horizontal distance from bearing at the ridge to bearing at the top plate (**Figure 68**).

To convert rafter span (horizontal distance) to rafter length (sloped distance), use the conversion factors in **Figure 3**, page 4.

Maximum rafter spans for common lumber species are given in **Figures 69 to 82**, pages 104-117.

Hip and Valley Rafters

While hip and valley rafters carry significant loads, they are often undersized. To allow for full bearing, hip and valley rafters should be at least one size larger than commons and jacks.

Sizing Hip and Valley Rafters

The loads on hip and valley rafters are *tributary loads* transferred from a wide area of the roof (**Figure 83**). The hip and valley rafter sizing table (**Figure 84**, page 50) accounts for such tributary loads.

Figure 68. Rafter Span

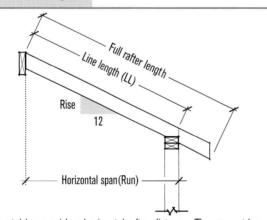

Rafter span tables provide a horizontal rafter distance. These must be multiplied by a line length ratio (**Figure 3,** page 4) to calculate a line length (sloping distance). Length for plumb cuts and overhang must be added to find full rafter length. Note: The rafter spans in the span tables (pages 104-117) have been shortened for the thickness of the ridge.

Figure 83. Calculating Tributary Load (W) on Hip and Valley Rafters

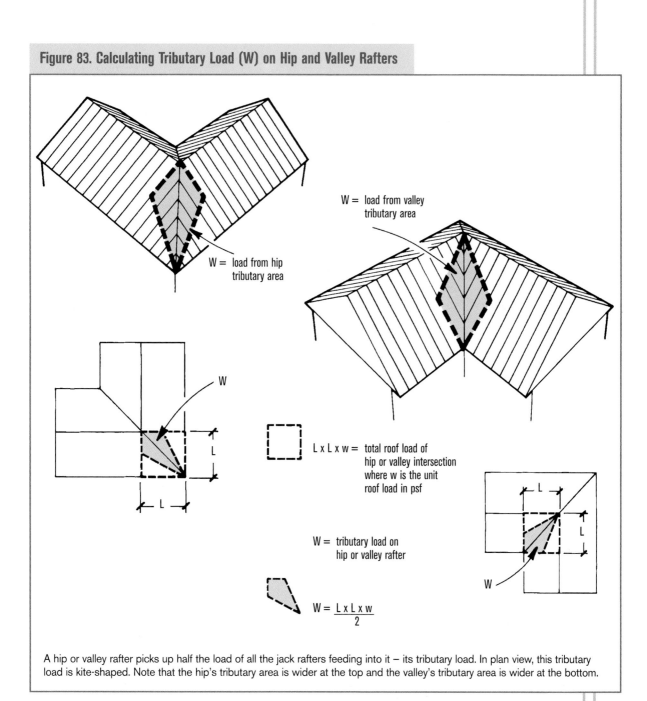

W = load from valley tributary area

W = load from hip tributary area

W

L

L

L x L x w = total roof load of hip or valley intersection where w is the unit roof load in psf

W = tributary load on hip or valley rafter

$$W = \frac{L \times L \times w}{2}$$

L

L

W

A hip or valley rafter picks up half the load of all the jack rafters feeding into it – its tributary load. In plan view, this tributary load is kite-shaped. Note that the hip's tributary area is wider at the top and the valley's tributary area is wider at the bottom.

Figure 84. Hip and Valley Rafter Sizing Table

L in feet	15 psf live load	30 psf live load	45 psf live load	60 psf live load
4	2x6	2x6	2x6	2x8*
5	2x6	2x6	2x6	2x8
6	2x6	2x8	2x8	2x10
7	2x8	2x10	2x10	2x12
8	2x10	2x12	2x12	(2) 2x12
9	2x10	(2) 2x12	(2) 2x12	(2) 2x12
10	2x12	(2) 2x12	(2) 2x12	LVL 11$7/8$
11	(2) 2x12	(2) 2x12	LVL 11$7/8$	LVL 11$7/8$
12	(2) 2x12	LVL 11$7/8$	LVL 11$7/8$	LVL 14
13	(2) 2x12	LVL 11$7/8$	LVL 14	(2) LVL 14
14	LVL 11$7/8$	LVL 14	(2) LVL 14	(2) LVL 14
15	LVL 11$7/8$	LVL 14	(2) LVL 14	(2) LVL 14
16	LVL 11$7/8$	(2) LVL 14	(2) LVL 14	(2) LVL 16*
17	LVL 14	(2) LVL 14	(2) LVL 16	(2) LVL 16
18	LVL 14	(2) LVL 14	(2) LVL 16	*
19	(2) LVL 14	(2) LVL 16*	*	–
20	(2) LVL 14	(2) LVL 16	–	–

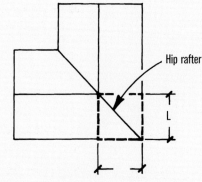

Hip rafter

L

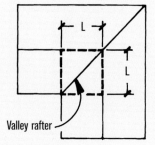

L

L

Valley rafter

*Deflection limited

Note: The calculations behind this table are based on the following:

10 psf dead load	F_b wood = 1,000 psi
L/240 deflection	E wood = 1,000,000 psi
No slope adjustments	F_b LVL = 2,800 psi
	E LVL = 2,000,000 psi

The table above summarizes a series of sizing calculations for various roof design loads. L represents the length of a hip or valley rafter for equally pitched roof intersections only.

Figure 85. Apex Support for Cathedral Ceiling Hips and Valleys

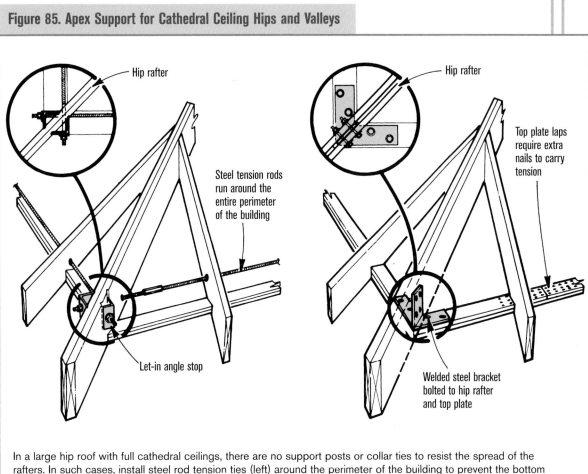

Hip rafter

Steel tension rods
run around the
entire perimeter
of the building

Let-in angle stop

Hip rafter

Top plate laps
require extra
nails to carry
tension

Welded steel bracket
bolted to hip rafter
and top plate

In a large hip roof with full cathedral ceilings, there are no support posts or collar ties to resist the spread of the rafters. In such cases, install steel rod tension ties (left) around the perimeter of the building to prevent the bottom ends of the hip rafters from spreading. Alternatively, use welded steel brackets to secure the hip rafters at the corners, allowing double 2x6 top plates to act as tension members (right).

Apex Support

In addition to choosing the right size hip or valley rafter, the point load at the high (ridge) end of a hip or valley must be well supported. Typically, common rafters tied together by ceiling joists or collar ties support this load. Large cathedral ceilings should be engineered to provide adequate support. This may include tension rods along the wall plates or reinforced plate connections for hip and valley rafters (**Figure 85**).

Rafter Bearing

Rafters should have bearing of at least $1^1/_2$ in. on the top plate or beam. Bearing should be on the heel of the rafter, not the toe. Bearing on the toe places most of the load on only a portion of the rafter and can lead to its splitting (**Figure 86**).

Figure 86. Rafter Bearing

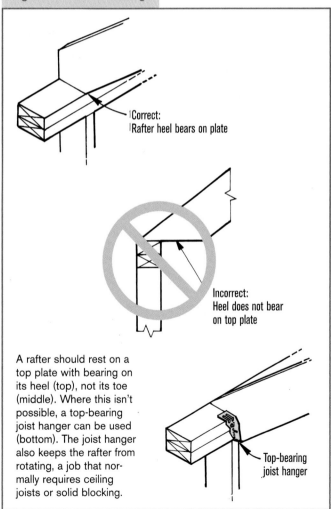

Correct:
Rafter heel bears on plate

Incorrect:
Heel does not bear
on top plate

Top-bearing
joist hanger

A rafter should rest on a top plate with bearing on its heel (top), not its toe (middle). Where this isn't possible, a top-bearing joist hanger can be used (bottom). The joist hanger also keeps the rafter from rotating, a job that normally requires ceiling joists or solid blocking.

A non-structural ridge board should be at least one size deeper than the common rafters to provide full bearing for the rafter's plumb cut.

Structural Bracing

Rafters must be restrained from spreading. This can be accomplished with adequate connections to ceiling joists, with collar ties, or with a structural ridge beam.

Rafter-Joist Connections

The connection between roof and wall at the eaves needs to resist uplift forces caused by wind (and earthquake activity in seismic zones), as well as horizontal thrust caused by roof loads. Low roof slopes, long rafter spans, and heavy snow loads increase horizontal thrust significantly.

Unless the roof has a structural ridge, the ceiling joists must be continuous across the building and must be fastened to the rafter tails with the number of nails shown in **Figure 87**. If the number of nails is excessive for the amount of nailing area, use bolts or framing clips instead.

A weak link in this system is where ceiling joists join at the center of a building. This connection requires the same nailing schedule as a collar tie-to-rafter

Figure 87. Nailing and Bolting Schedule for Eaves Tie Connections

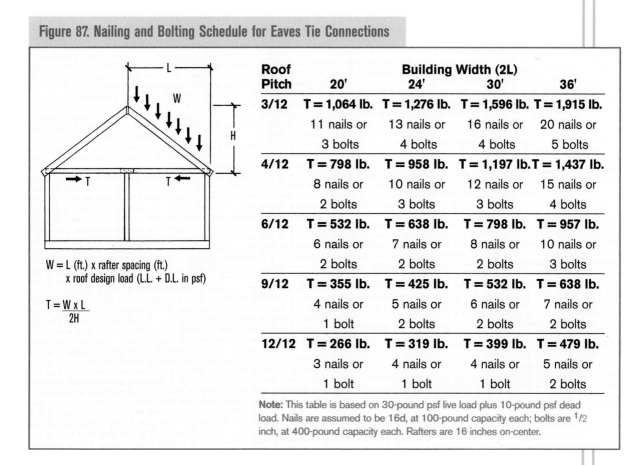

Roof Pitch	Building Width (2L) 20'	24'	30'	36'
3/12	T = 1,064 lb.	T = 1,276 lb.	T = 1,596 lb.	T = 1,915 lb.
	11 nails or	13 nails or	16 nails or	20 nails or
	3 bolts	4 bolts	4 bolts	5 bolts
4/12	T = 798 lb.	T = 958 lb.	T = 1,197 lb.	T = 1,437 lb.
	8 nails or	10 nails or	12 nails or	15 nails or
	2 bolts	3 bolts	3 bolts	4 bolts
6/12	T = 532 lb.	T = 638 lb.	T = 798 lb.	T = 957 lb.
	6 nails or	7 nails or	8 nails or	10 nails or
	2 bolts	2 bolts	2 bolts	3 bolts
9/12	T = 355 lb.	T = 425 lb.	T = 532 lb.	T = 638 lb.
	4 nails or	5 nails or	6 nails or	7 nails or
	1 bolt	2 bolts	2 bolts	2 bolts
12/12	T = 266 lb.	T = 319 lb.	T = 399 lb.	T = 479 lb.
	3 nails or	4 nails or	4 nails or	5 nails or
	1 bolt	1 bolt	1 bolt	2 bolts

W = L (ft.) x rafter spacing (ft.)
x roof design load (L.L. + D.L. in psf)

$$T = \frac{W \times L}{2H}$$

Note: This table is based on 30-pound psf live load plus 10-pound psf dead load. Nails are assumed to be 16d, at 100-pound capacity each; bolts are 1/2 inch, at 400-pound capacity each. Rafters are 16 inches on-center.

Figure 88. Connecting Flush-Framed Ceiling Joists

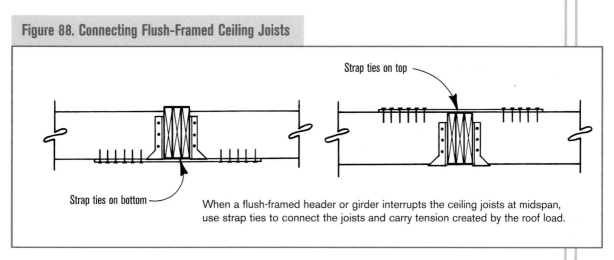

Strap ties on top

Strap ties on bottom

When a flush-framed header or girder interrupts the ceiling joists at midspan, use strap ties to connect the joists and carry tension created by the roof load.

Figure 89. Placing Collar Ties

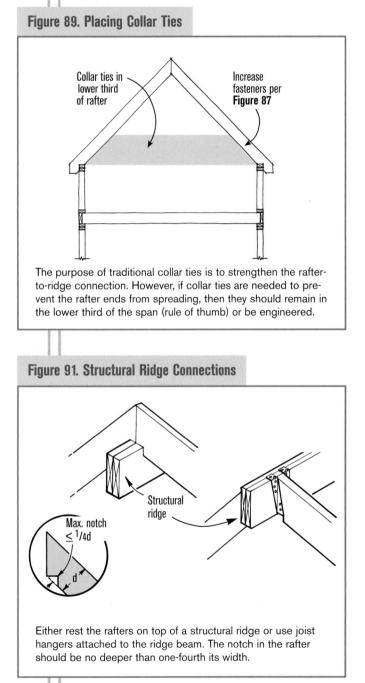

Collar ties in lower third of rafter

Increase fasteners per **Figure 87**

The purpose of traditional collar ties is to strengthen the rafter-to-ridge connection. However, if collar ties are needed to prevent the rafter ends from spreading, then they should remain in the lower third of the span (rule of thumb) or be engineered.

Figure 91. Structural Ridge Connections

Structural ridge

Max. notch ≤ $^1/_4$d

Either rest the rafters on top of a structural ridge or use joist hangers attached to the ridge beam. The notch in the rafter should be no deeper than one-fourth its width.

connection (**Figure 16**, pages 16-17). When the ceiling joists are in the same plane, as with a flush-framed beam, steel strap ties can be used (**Figure 88**).

Collar Ties

Collar ties often are placed near the ridge, but this placement only serves to strengthen the rafter-to-ridge connection and to stiffen the rafters. To effectively keep rafters from spreading, collar ties must be in the lower third of the rafter (**Figure 89**). They are not necessary if the rafters are adequately nailed to ceiling joists.

Collar-tie connections should be treated like rafter-to-joist connections (**Figure 87**, previous page).

Structural Ridge Beams

In a cathedral ceiling, the outward thrust of rafters is not restrained by ceiling joists or rafter ties and the rafter tops must bear on a structural ridge beam. Sizing for structural ridge beams is shown in **Figure 90**.

Rafters may sit on top of a structural ridge or may be supported by joist hangers or anchors (**Figure 91**).

Purlins and Roof Struts

Purlins and struts can be used to reduce rafter spans or to stiffen rafters (**Figure 92**). To properly support the roof, the purlins should be at least the same dimension as the rafters while the struts should transfer the load to a bearing wall at an angle not less than 45 degrees. The IRC 2000 sets the maximum spacing of 2x4 struts at 4 ft. o.c.

Figure 92. Purlin Design

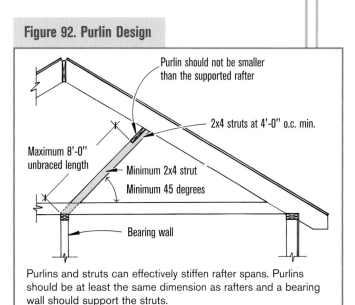

Purlin should not be smaller than the supported rafter

2x4 struts at 4'-0" o.c. min.

Maximum 8'-0" unbraced length

Minimum 2x4 strut

Minimum 45 degrees

Bearing wall

Purlins and struts can effectively stiffen rafter spans. Purlins should be at least the same dimension as rafters and a bearing wall should support the struts.

Figure 90. Structural Ridge Beam Spans for 20 psf Roof Live Load

| | Roof Dead Load = 10 psf | | | Roof Dead Load = 20 psf | | |
| | Building Width (ft.) | | | Building Width (ft.) | | |
	20	28	36	20	28	36
Size	**Maximum Ridge Beam Spans for Common Lumber Species (ft.-in.)***					
1-2x6	4-10	4-1	3-7	4-2	3-6	3-1
1-2x8	6-1	5-2	4-7	5-3	4-6	3-11
1-2x10	7-5	6-4	5-7	6-5	5-5	4-10
1-2x12	8-8	7-4	6-5	7-6	6-4	5-7
2-2x6	7-2	6-0	5-4	6-2	5-3	4-7
2-2x8	9-1	7-8	6-9	7-10	6-7	5-10
2-2x10	11-1	9-4	8-3	9-7	8-1	7-2
2-2x12	12-10	10-10	9-7	11-1	9-5	8-3
3-2x8	11-1	9-7	8-5	9-10	8-4	7-4
3-2x10	13-10	11-8	10-4	12-0	10-2	8-11
3-2x12	16-1	13-7	12-0	13-11	11-9	10-4
4-2x8	12-3	10-11	9-9	11-1	9-7	8-5
4-2x10	15-7	13-6	11-11	13-10	11-8	10-4

* Tabulated values assume #2 Grade Douglas Fir-Larch, Hem-Fir, Southern Pine, or Spruce-Pine-Fir lumber.

Cathedral ceilings require structural ridge beams. This table shows two dead loading conditions (10 and 20 psf) under live load conditions of 20 psf. In areas with heavier snow and wind live loads, stronger ridge beams will be required. For longer spans and heavier loading conditions, consider using LVL or other engineered materials.

Figure 93. Raised-Rafter-Plate Connections

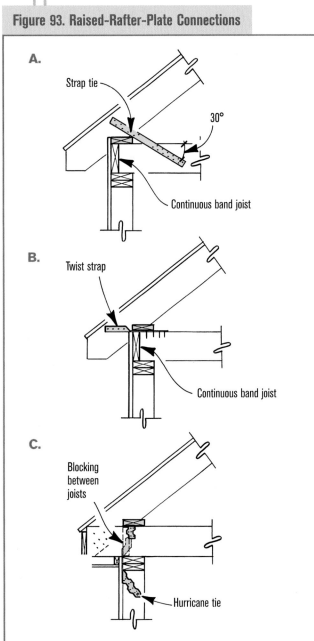

Using rated strap ties (A) is an effective way to resist roof thrust and uplift on raised rafters. When an attic floor is in the way, twist straps (B) will work, but may require additional wind ties in high wind areas. Extending the attic joist beyond the wall (C) allows for hurricane ties to help resist uplift.

Raised Rafter Plates

To create added space for insulation at the eaves, many builders raise the rafters up and fasten them to a plate nailed to the top of the ceiling joists.

While this reduces heat loss and ice dams, it also weakens the important connection between the ceiling joists and the rafter ends, thereby requiring reinforcement (**Figure 93**).

Blocking for End Restraint

Rafter ends connected to ceiling joists are generally not at risk of rotating. But where rafters sit on a beam or plate by themselves or are raised above the joists, full-height blocking should be installed between the rafters or a rim joist (or subfascia) should be nailed to their ends.

Blocking is often needed to close off open eaves (no soffit), but not for structural reasons.

Overhangs

In general, roof overhangs should not exceed 2 ft. or one-third the horizontal span of the rafter, whichever is less (**Figure 94**).

Rake Overhangs

There are two common ways to build overhangs at rakes:

- For overhangs shorter than 1 ft., blocks nailed to the gable-end wall are adequate.
- For larger overhangs, short "out-lookers," or purlins, are typically cantilevered (**Figure 95**). These should not cantilever more than 2 ft. or half the span of the purlin, whichever is less.

Roof Openings

In general, at roof openings more than 4 ft. wide, both headers and trimmers should be doubled. At openings more than 6 ft. wide, joist hangers should support headers unless they bear on a supporting beam or wall.

Figure 94. Roof Overhangs

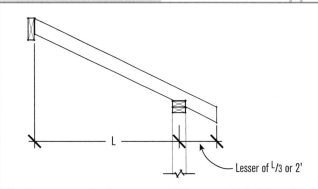

Lesser of $L/3$ or 2'

Roof overhangs should not exceed 2 ft. or one-third of the rafter span, whichever is less.

Figure 95. Rake Overhangs

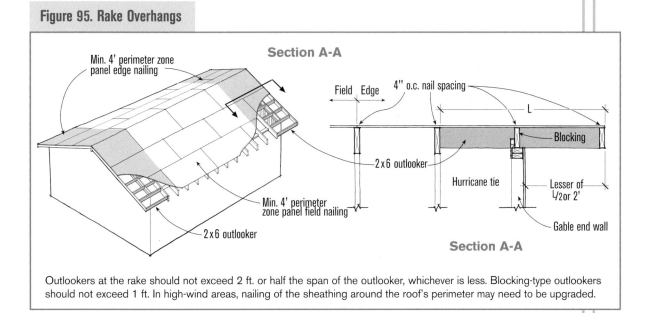

Outlookers at the rake should not exceed 2 ft. or half the span of the outlooker, whichever is less. Blocking-type outlookers should not exceed 1 ft. In high-wind areas, nailing of the sheathing around the roof's perimeter may need to be upgraded.

Shed Dormers

Adding a shed dormer to a typical gable roof upsets the balance of forces by breaking the stable triangle formed by the rafters and ceiling joists.

Two common ways to support the dormer loads are with a center loadbearing wall (**Figure 96**) or a structural ridge. Either solution must provide a continuous load path to the foundation.

Shed Dormers With Structural Ridges

A structural ridge can replace the ridge or can be installed beneath it (**Figure 97**).

Figure 96. Center Support for Shed Dormers

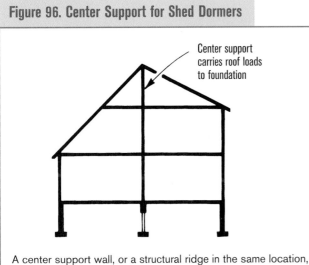

Center support carries roof loads to foundation

A center support wall, or a structural ridge in the same location, will handle the unbalanced loads caused by adding a shed dormer. The loads must follow a continuous path to the footing.

Figure 97. Retrofit Ridge Connections for Shed Dormers

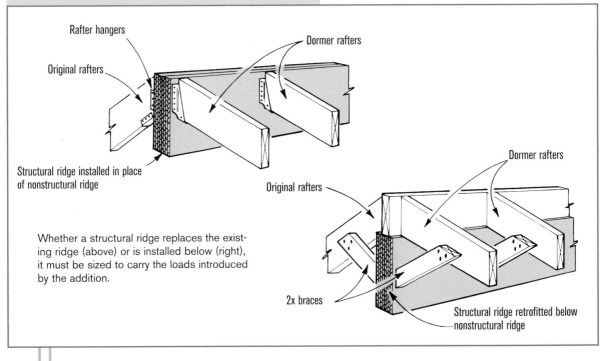

Rafter hangers

Original rafters

Dormer rafters

Structural ridge installed in place of nonstructural ridge

Whether a structural ridge replaces the existing ridge (above) or is installed below (right), it must be sized to carry the loads introduced by the addition.

Dormer rafters

Original rafters

2x braces

Structural ridge retrofitted below nonstructural ridge

Figure 98. Dropped-Ridge Dormer (with Structural Ridge)

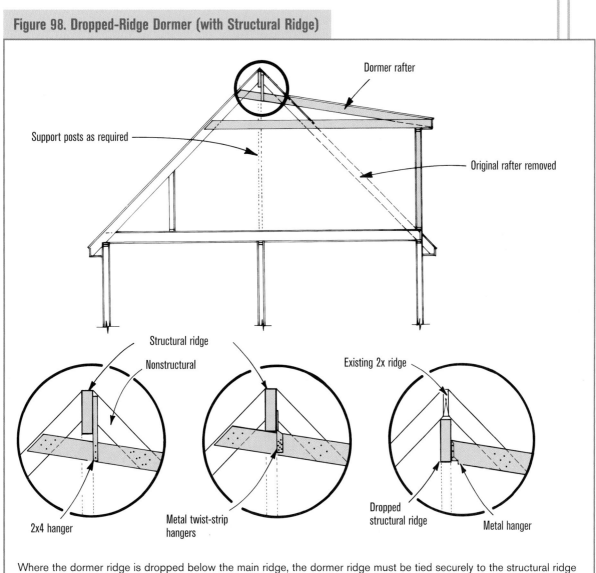

Dormer rafter

Support posts as required

Original rafter removed

Structural ridge

Nonstructural

Existing 2x ridge

2x4 hanger

Metal twist-strip hangers

Dropped structural ridge

Metal hanger

Where the dormer ridge is dropped below the main ridge, the dormer ridge must be tied securely to the structural ridge or center loadbearing wall. Several options are shown.

Where a structural dormer ridge is dropped, it should tie in securely to the structural ridge or center loadbearing wall (**Figure 98**).

With no structural ridge or center loadbearing walls, small shed dormers are still possible but a combination of structural elements must be added (**Figure 99**, page 60).

Figure 99. Precautions for Small Shed Dormers

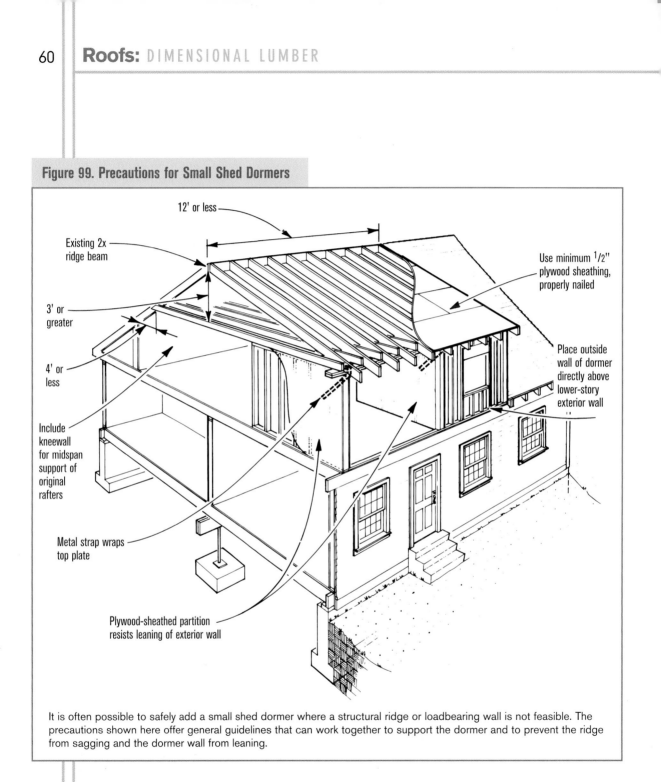

12' or less

Existing 2x ridge beam

Use minimum $1/2''$ plywood sheathing, properly nailed

3' or greater

4' or less

Place outside wall of dormer directly above lower-story exterior wall

Include kneewall for midspan support of original rafters

Metal strap wraps top plate

Plywood-sheathed partition resists leaning of exterior wall

It is often possible to safely add a small shed dormer where a structural ridge or loadbearing wall is not feasible. The precautions shown here offer general guidelines that can work together to support the dormer and to prevent the ridge from sagging and the dormer wall from leaning.

Roofs: WOOD I-BEAMS

I-beams are being used more often in roof framing, particularly on cathedral-type ceilings with long spans.

Structural Ridge Required

All I-beam roofs require a center load-bearing wall or a structural ridge beam, since there is no practical way to make a strong shear connection at the rafter ends to resist horizontal thrust.

Structural Ridge With Hangers

The most common connection at the ridge is a face-mounted hanger with a sloped seat. These hangers can be adjusted in the field to match the I-beam slope, and can be skewed side-to-side up to 45 degrees for hip and valley jack rafters.

Install beveled web-stiffeners on each side of an I-beam where it sits in the hanger. Leave a $1/8$- to $1/4$-in. gap at the top flange and secure the stiffeners by driving three or more 8d nails from each side, staggered and with the points clinched. Larger I-beams may require 2x stiffeners with 16d nails. In

Figure 101. Structural Ridge Connections

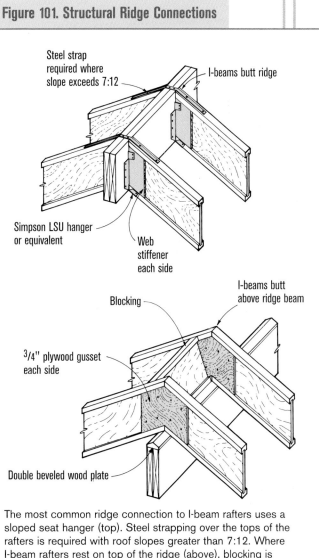

Steel strap required where slope exceeds 7:12

I-beams butt ridge

Simpson LSU hanger or equivalent

Web stiffener each side

Blocking

I-beams butt above ridge beam

$3/4$" plywood gusset each side

Double beveled wood plate

The most common ridge connection to I-beam rafters uses a sloped seat hanger (top). Steel strapping over the tops of the rafters is required with roof slopes greater than 7:12. Where I-beam rafters rest on top of the ridge (above), blocking is required on both sides of the ridge.

Figure 102. Birdsmouth Cut for I-Beam Rafters

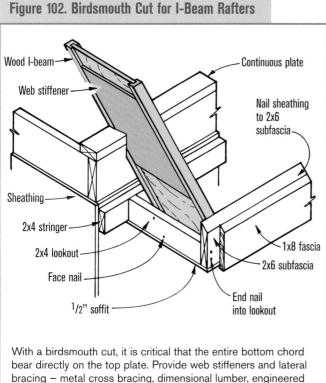

Wood I-beam

Web stiffener

Continuous plate

Nail sheathing to 2x6 subfascia

Sheathing

2x4 stringer

2x4 lookout

Face nail

1/2" soffit

1x8 fascia

2x6 subfascia

End nail into lookout

With a birdsmouth cut, it is critical that the entire bottom chord bear directly on the top plate. Provide web stiffeners and lateral bracing – metal cross bracing, dimensional lumber, engineered rim joist material, or I-beam material – on both sides of rafter.

all cases, follow manufacturers' nailing schedules.

Structural Ridge Below Rafters

I-beams can sit on top of a structural ridge on a beveled plate (**Figure 101**, previous page). Never cut a birds-mouth in the I-beam at the ridge — this would require cutting though the bottom flange, thereby damaging the joist.

To prevent rafters from rolling, install blocking between the I-beams on

either side of the ridge. The blocking can be I-beam material, dimensional lumber, or metal cross-bracing. If you need to leave room for a ventilation channel, use dimensional lumber or engineered rim joist material notched to allow airflow, or use metal cross-bracing.

Eaves Connections

A number of details are possible at the exterior wall plate, depending on the roof profile desired.

Birdsmouth for I-Beam Rafters

The most common approach to joining I-beam rafters to walls is to cut a birdsmouth at the plate. The seat must never overhang the inside face of the bearing wall, otherwise the I-beam will be compromised. Web stiffeners are required on both sides of the birdsmouth cut (**Figure 102**).

Beveled Wall Plates for I-Beam Rafters

I-joist rafters can sit on a beveled top plate (**Figure 103**). This option can save time since no birdsmouth or web stiffeners are required.

Blocking between rafters is required when using beveled wall plates. For blocking, use either I-beams, dimensional lumber, or metal cross-bracing.

Some I-beam manufacturers may require additional connectors on roofs with steep slopes.

Sloped Seat Connectors

A third option to connect I-beam rafters to walls is to use sloped-seat metal connectors. As with the beveled-plate approach, these do not require a birdsmouth or web stiffeners, but do require blocking between rafters.

I-Beam Overhangs

Because cutting through the bottom flange compromises the strength of an I-beam rafter, rafter tails with birdsmouths are limited to a 2-ft. horizontal projection (**Figure 104**).

Soffits

There are several ways to build traditional soffits. One common approach is to attach 2x4 blocking to the I-beam rafter tails as shown in **Figure 102**. Another option is to sister on rafter tails of dimensional lumber.

Gable-End Overhangs

For an overhang at the gable end, cantilever dimensional lumber outriggers across the rake-wall top plate (**Figure 105**). These are similar to the outriggers used in stick framing (**Figure 95**, page 57).

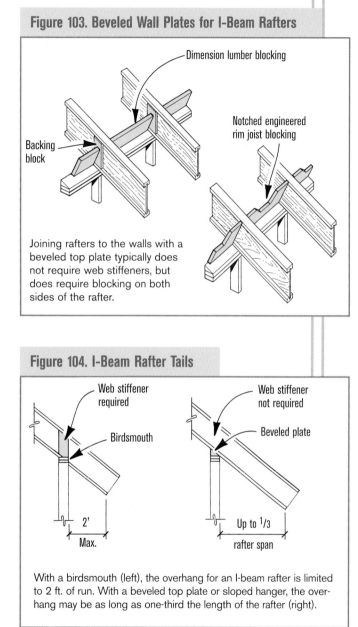

Figure 103. Beveled Wall Plates for I-Beam Rafters

Dimension lumber blocking

Notched engineered rim joist blocking

Backing block

Joining rafters to the walls with a beveled top plate typically does not require web stiffeners, but does require blocking on both sides of the rafter.

Figure 104. I-Beam Rafter Tails

Web stiffener required

Web stiffener not required

Birdsmouth

Beveled plate

2'
Max.

Up to $1/3$
rafter span

With a birdsmouth (left), the overhang for an I-beam rafter is limited to 2 ft. of run. With a beveled top plate or sloped hanger, the overhang may be as long as one-third the length of the rafter (right).

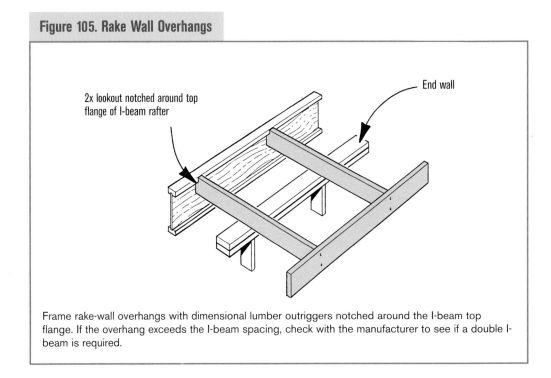

Figure 105. Rake Wall Overhangs

2x lookout notched around top
flange of I-beam rafter

End wall

Frame rake-wall overhangs with dimensional lumber outriggers notched around the I-beam top flange. If the overhang exceeds the I-beam spacing, check with the manufacturer to see if a double I-beam is required.

Temporary Bracing for I-Beams

I-beam rafters (like floor I-joists) are unstable until fully braced and sheathed. It's crucial to install all blocking and provide lateral restraint before applying any weight to the rafters. As with floor I-joists, stabilize an unbraced end by installing the first 4 ft. of sheathing, then brace the rest of the rafters with 1x4 braces nailed flat to the top of the I-beam rafters every 6 to 8 ft. and lapped at the ends by at least two joists.

Roofs: TRUSSES

The main components of a truss are shown in **Figure 106**. Roofs framed with trusses are engineered systems. They must be installed and braced properly to work as planned. Any changes from the original plan in bearing or loading or any field modifications to the trusses must be engineered.

Truss Types

Many types of standard trusses are now produced and almost any roof design can be custom fabricated. The most popular types of trusses are shown in **Figure 107**.

Truss Overhangs

When ordering trusses, specify the span, slope, width of the bearing walls (2x4 or 2x6), and the length and type of overhang (**Figure 108**).

Figure 106. Truss Components

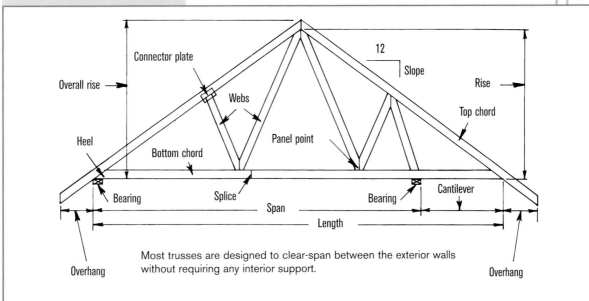

Most trusses are designed to clear-span between the exterior walls without requiring any interior support.

Figure 107. Truss Types

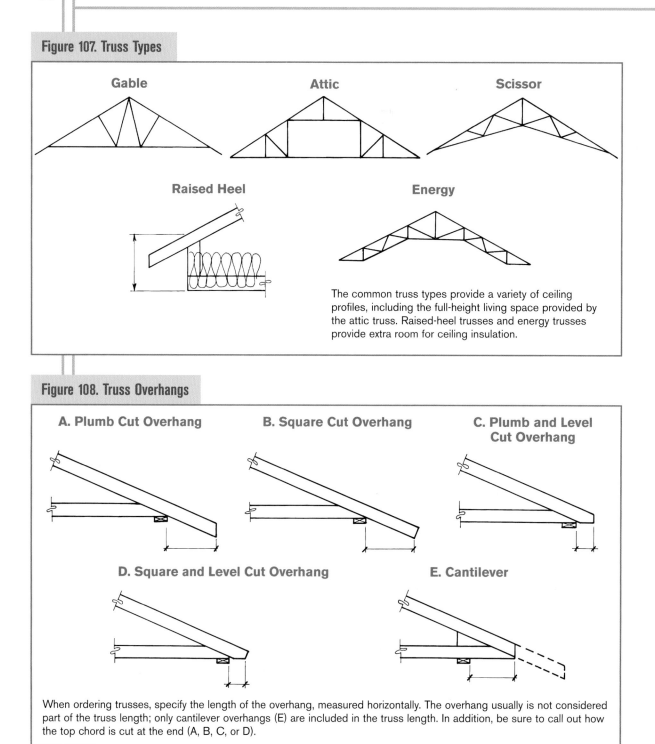

The common truss types provide a variety of ceiling profiles, including the full-height living space provided by the attic truss. Raised-heel trusses and energy trusses provide extra room for ceiling insulation.

Figure 108. Truss Overhangs

When ordering trusses, specify the length of the overhang, measured horizontally. The overhang usually is not considered part of the truss length; only cantilever overhangs (E) are included in the truss length. In addition, be sure to call out how the top chord is cut at the end (A, B, C, or D).

Figure 109. Truss Hip Anatomy

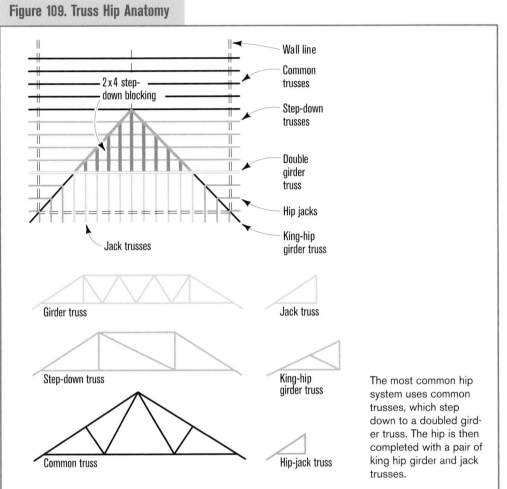

Wall line

Common trusses

2 x 4 step-down blocking

Step-down trusses

Double girder truss

Hip jacks

King-hip girder truss

Jack trusses

Girder truss

Jack truss

Step-down truss

King-hip girder truss

Common truss

Hip-jack truss

The most common hip system uses common trusses, which step down to a doubled girder truss. The hip is then completed with a pair of king hip girder and jack trusses.

The truss length is typically the length of the bottom chord; it does not include the overhang, which is most often a projection of the top chord.

Hip and Valley Trusses

Hip roofs and valleys between intersecting roofs may be built around an assembly of jack trusses attached to a girder truss.

Hips. Step-down trusses complete the upper end of the hip series and smaller trusses fill in the lower corners (**Figure 109**). As with other trusses, it's critical that the dimensions of the building match the drawing and that walls are square and level.

Valleys on a trussed roof are usually framed conventionally. However, when a project includes more than one valley of the same size, a valley set may be more economical (**Figure 110**).

Figure 110. Valley Sets

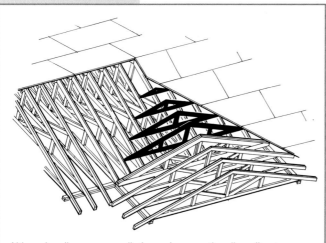

Although valleys are usually framed conventionally, valley truss systems may be more economical if the same size valley is used more than once in a project.

Figure 111. Lifting Trusses

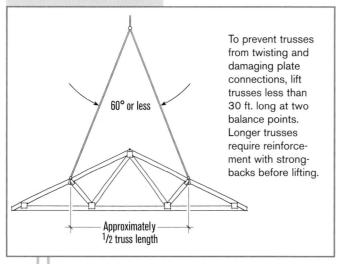

60° or less

To prevent trusses from twisting and damaging plate connections, lift trusses less than 30 ft. long at two balance points. Longer trusses require reinforcement with strongbacks before lifting.

Approximately 1/2 truss length

The Essential Guide to Framing

Handling and Storing Trusses

Trusses are vulnerable to damage until they are installed, sheathed, and braced. To prevent damage, use the following precautions:

- Inspect trusses when receiving a shipment. Look carefully for loose plates and reject any damaged trusses.

- Banded trusses should be lifted off the truck from two points on the top chords. Individual trusses should be lifted the same way (**Figure 111**).

- Store trusses horizontally on relatively level, dry ground. To prevent any bending or twisting that could loosen truss plates, support the trusses with blocking placed every 8- to 10-ft.

- If trusses must be stored vertically, make sure they are braced and blocked in a stable manner. Gable trusses should be stored with their peaks up, scissors trusses with their peaks down.

Bracing Roof Trusses

Trusses are inherently unstable until sheathed and require two types of bracing: temporary and permanent.

Use temporary bracing to safely erect the trusses; permanent bracing is required to stabilize the trusses throughout the life of the structure. The truss fabricator or "designer of record" should provide a permanent bracing plan.

Usually some of the elements of the temporary bracing stay in place as part of the permanent bracing. In general, all bracing should be placed near panel points (where truss members meet).

Temporary Bracing: The First Truss

It is important to accurately plumb the first truss and to brace it substantially, since additional trusses rely on the first one for stability.

All bracing must be of 2x material.

Start with the gable-end truss. Most builders start by sheathing the gable-end

Figure 112. Bracing to the Deck

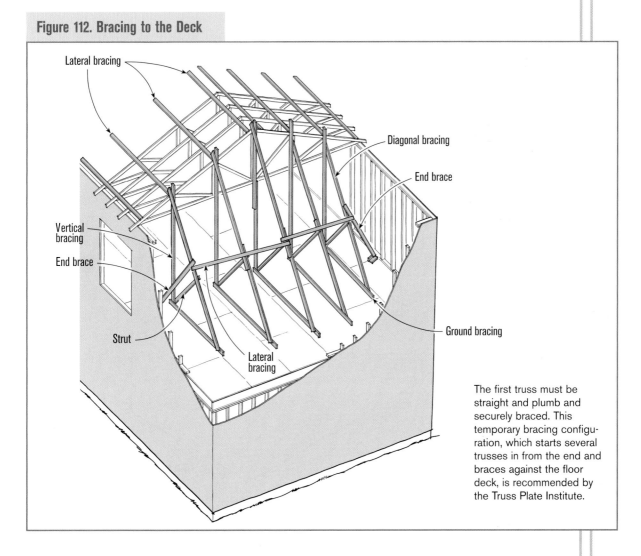

The first truss must be straight and plumb and securely braced. This temporary bracing configuration, which starts several trusses in from the end and braces against the floor deck, is recommended by the Truss Plate Institute.

Figure 113. Bracing to the End Wall

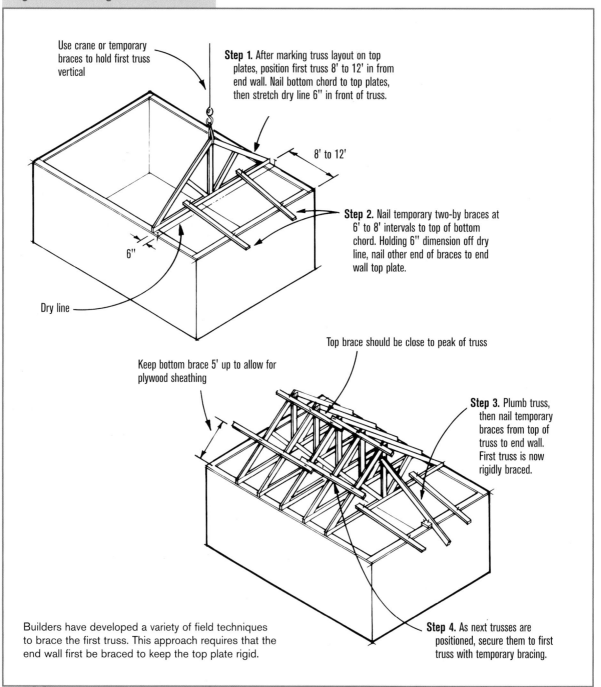

Use crane or temporary braces to hold first truss vertical

Step 1. After marking truss layout on top plates, position first truss 8' to 12' in from end wall. Nail bottom chord to top plates, then stretch dry line 6" in front of truss.

8' to 12'

6"

Dry line

Step 2. Nail temporary two-by braces at 6' to 8' intervals to top of bottom chord. Holding 6" dimension off dry line, nail other end of braces to end wall top plate.

Top brace should be close to peak of truss

Keep bottom brace 5' up to allow for plywood sheathing

Step 3. Plumb truss, then nail temporary braces from top of truss to end wall. First truss is now rigidly braced.

Builders have developed a variety of field techniques to brace the first truss. This approach requires that the end wall first be braced to keep the top plate rigid.

Step 4. As next trusses are positioned, secure them to first truss with temporary bracing.

truss on the ground and lifting that first. Unfortunately, the gable-end truss is difficult to brace back to the deck without the braces interfering with the second truss. On a one-story building, the gable-end truss can be braced to stakes driven in the ground.

Start several trusses in. Alternatively, start the first truss 8- to 12-ft. in from the gable end and brace it to the deck (**Figure 112**, page 69). Then work away from the braced end, filling in the open 8- to 12-ft. section last, after permanently bracing the rest of the trusses.

Or brace the trusses to an end wall (**Figure 113**). It may first be necessary to solidly brace the end wall to the deck to keep the top plate rigid.

Temporary Bracing: Subsequent Trusses

Spacers. As trusses are added to the roof, they can be spaced from the preceding truss with short 1x4 or 2x4 spacers pre-cut to length, with light-gauge metal spacers or with heavy-duty fold-out metal braces. (The heavy metal braces can also serve as temporary lateral bracing for the top chord.)

Top-chord bracing. As soon as the fourth truss is up, start fastening lateral bracing across the top chords — one brace near the peak and one near the midpoint of each top chord. If

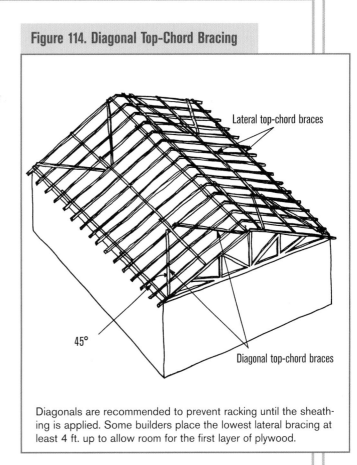

Figure 114. Diagonal Top-Chord Bracing

Lateral top-chord braces

45°

Diagonal top-chord braces

Diagonals are recommended to prevent racking until the sheathing is applied. Some builders place the lowest lateral bracing at least 4 ft. up to allow room for the first layer of plywood.

required, place diagonal bracing at each end of the roof and at 20-ft. intervals in between (**Figure 114**).

All lateral bracing should be minimum construction-grade 2x4s, at least 10 ft. long and nailed with two 16d nails at each intersection. Individual pieces should lap at least one bay.

Roof sheathing. To quickly stabilize the top chords, some builders start installing sheathing after about a dozen trusses have been installed. The sheathing acts as both temporary and permanent bracing for the top chords.

To simplify installation of the sheathing, some builders keep the lower top-chord braces 5 ft. up from the eaves line to allow room for the first course of sheathing. Unless the sheathing is installed shortly after erecting the trusses, diagonal top-chord braces may be needed to prevent racking in the roof or truss collapse.

Bottom-chord bracing. After the fourth truss is up, also start installing lateral bracing on the bottom chord (along its top edge if the bottom chords are receiving drywall). Install bottom-chord bracing according to the permanent bracing plan and leave in place. On large trusses, diagonal bottom-chord bracing may be required at each end and at 20-ft. intervals in between.

Web cross-bracing. After the fourth truss is up, also start fastening diagonal cross-bracing to the vertical webs. Cross-bracing of the vertical webs goes in an X pattern at each end of the building and every 20 ft. in between (**Figure 115**). Install web cross-bracing according to the permanent bracing plan and leave in place.

Figure 115. Bottom-Chord Bracing and Web Cross-Bracing

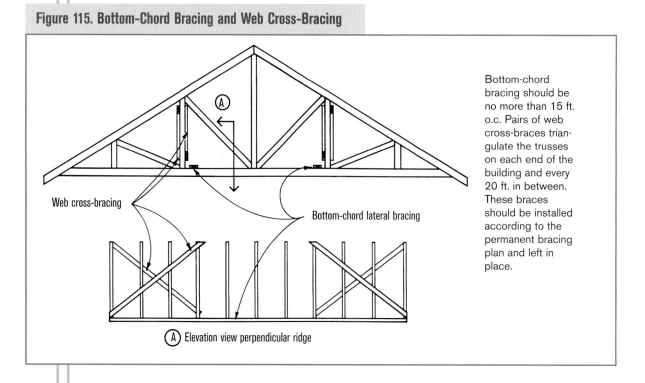

Web cross-bracing

Bottom-chord lateral bracing

(A) Elevation view perpendicular ridge

Bottom-chord bracing should be no more than 15 ft. o.c. Pairs of web cross-braces triangulate the trusses on each end of the building and every 20 ft. in between. These braces should be installed according to the permanent bracing plan and left in place.

Figure 116. Bracing Piggyback Trusses

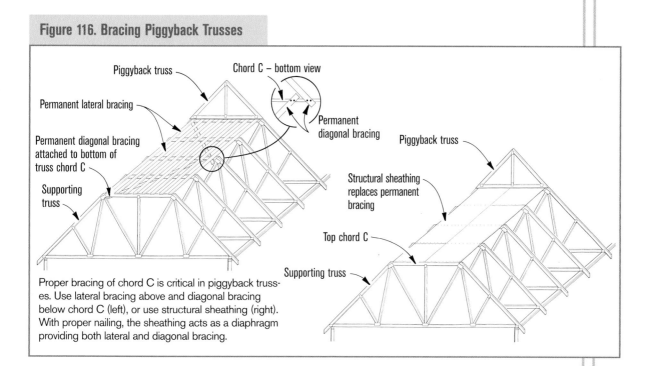

Piggyback truss

Chord C – bottom view

Permanent lateral bracing

Permanent diagonal bracing

Permanent diagonal bracing attached to bottom of truss chord C

Piggyback truss

Structural sheathing replaces permanent bracing

Supporting truss

Top chord C

Supporting truss

Proper bracing of chord C is critical in piggyback trusses. Use lateral bracing above and diagonal bracing below chord C (left), or use structural sheathing (right). With proper nailing, the sheathing acts as a diaphragm providing both lateral and diagonal bracing.

Permanent Truss Bracing

To perform as designed, roof trusses require permanent bracing after assembly, as specified by the "designer of record" on the job. In the absence of an architect or engineer, this responsibility may fall to the general contractor.

Permanent bracing typically consists of many of the same elements as the temporary bracing (see above), most of which are left in place after construction. One exception is any top-chord bracing, which must be removed to allow installation of the roof sheathing. The roof sheathing then serves as permanent top-chord bracing.

Piggyback Trusses

When trusses exceed 12- to 14-ft. in height, they are typically shipped in two sections to comply with highway transportation limits. These so-called "piggyback trusses" have special bracing requirements. Ignoring these requirements can lead to catastrophic failure under heavy loads such as snow.

In particular, it is critical to stabilize the top chords of the lower truss sections with either plywood or diagonal bracing (**Figure 116**). Other permanent bracing may also be required.

Framing: SEISMIC AND WIND BRACING

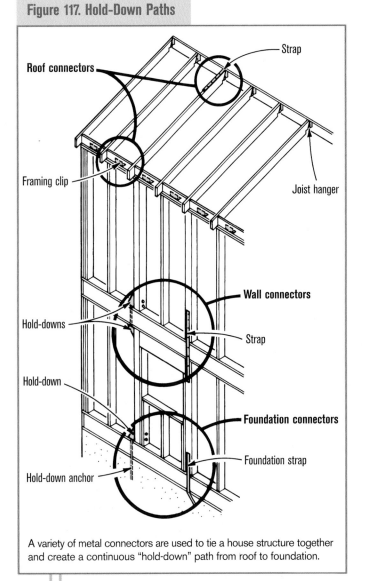

Strap

Roof connectors

Framing clip

Joist hanger

Wall connectors

Hold-downs

Strap

Hold-down

Foundation connectors

Foundation strap

Hold-down anchor

A variety of metal connectors are used to tie a house structure together and create a continuous "hold-down" path from roof to foundation.

High winds exert strong lateral forces on walls and uplift forces on roofs. Earthquakes also exert strong lateral forces, along with vertical shaking and other damaging forces. To help buildings in affected areas resist these forces, codes require that they have sufficient shear strength and have a continuous "hold down" path from roof to foundation (**Figure 117**). Metal connectors are typically required at the weak points between foundation and first floor, at level changes, and where upper walls join roofs. The details and hardware needed are similar in both seismic and high-wind areas.

Shear Walls

Continuous plywood across wall planes and tighter nailing schedules are crucial elements of structural design for seismic and high-wind areas.

Shear Wall Nailing

Shear walls are designed to resist racking. Both interior and exterior shear walls have rigorous nailing schedules,

Figure 118. Typical Shear Wall Details

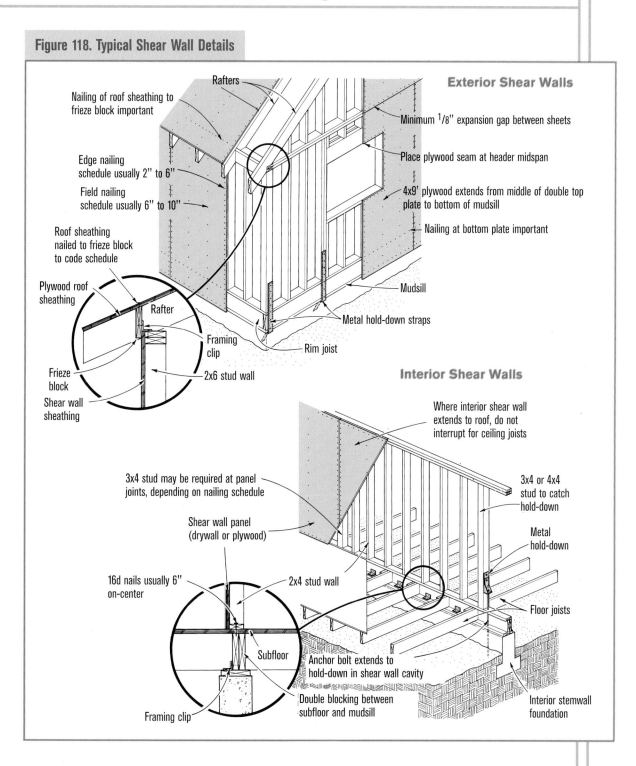

Rafters

Nailing of roof sheathing to frieze block important

Exterior Shear Walls

Minimum $1/8''$ expansion gap between sheets

Edge nailing schedule usually 2" to 6"

Place plywood seam at header midspan

Field nailing schedule usually 6" to 10"

4x9' plywood extends from middle of double top plate to bottom of mudsill

Roof sheathing nailed to frieze block to code schedule

Nailing at bottom plate important

Plywood roof sheathing

Rafter

Framing clip

Mudsill

Frieze block

2x6 stud wall

Metal hold-down straps

Shear wall sheathing

Rim joist

Interior Shear Walls

Where interior shear wall extends to roof, do not interrupt for ceiling joists

3x4 stud may be required at panel joints, depending on nailing schedule

3x4 or 4x4 stud to catch hold-down

Shear wall panel (drywall or plywood)

Metal hold-down

16d nails usually 6" on-center

2x4 stud wall

Subfloor

Floor joists

Anchor bolt extends to hold-down in shear wall cavity

Framing clip

Double blocking between subfloor and mudsill

Interior stemwall foundation

Figure 119. Proper Nailing at Shear Panel Joints

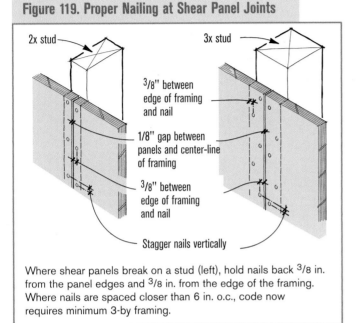

2x stud

3x stud

3/8" between edge of framing and nail

1/8" gap between panels and center-line of framing

3/8" between edge of framing and nail

Stagger nails vertically

Where shear panels break on a stud (left), hold nails back 3/8 in. from the panel edges and 3/8 in. from the edge of the framing. Where nails are spaced closer than 6 in. o.c., code now requires minimum 3-by framing.

Figure 120. Shear Wall Boundaries

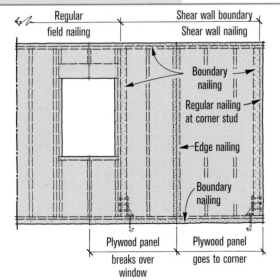

Regular field nailing

Shear wall boundary
Shear wall nailing

Boundary nailing

Regular nailing at corner stud

Edge nailing

Boundary nailing

Plywood panel breaks over window

Plywood panel goes to corner

Where plywood edges fall within the shear wall boundary, 3-by framing is required to prevent splitting from the close nailing pattern. Where a plywood edge falls outside the shear wall boundary, however, as at the window opening, standard sheathing nailing is permitted.

with nails spaced only 2- to 3-in. apart on panel edges (**Figure 118**, previous page). Nails must be held back 3/8 in. from the edges of sheathing panels and 3/8 in. in from the edges of framing members. Also, they must be staggered vertically (**Figure 119**).

Nail types and sizes are also specified. While galvanized nails can be used, they have lower shear values and require larger nails or closer spacing.

Nail heads must be large enough and must not be over-driven (**Figure 121**).

Shear Wall Blocking

Because shear forces are transferred at panel edges, all edges of plywood and other sheathing panels must be fastened to solid blocking. Many builders use 4x9 or 4x10 plywood panels installed vertically (**Figure 118**, previous page).

Where sheathing panels meet, each edge must have at least 1/2 in. of bearing on the stud, plate, or other member it is nailed to. Where the design shear exceeds 350 lbs. per foot (typically, where nails are spaced closer than 6 in. o.c.), the Uniform Building Code requires minimum 3x lumber at the joint. Most builders use 4x4s (**Figure 120**).

Figure 121. Setting Nails

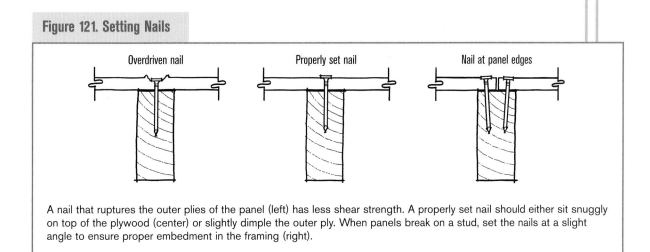

Overdriven nail | Properly set nail | Nail at panel edges

A nail that ruptures the outer plies of the panel (left) has less shear strength. A properly set nail should either sit snuggly on top of the plywood (center) or slightly dimple the outer ply. When panels break on a stud, set the nails at a slight angle to ensure proper embedment in the framing (right).

Anchoring to Foundations

All shear walls must be mechanically fastened to the foundation with metal hold-downs, metal straps, closed-space anchor bolts, or some combination of these.

Hold-Downs

These L-shaped brackets attach to anchor posts (anchor bolts) embedded in the foundation. For studs in a wall without openings, it's often best to install the studs that connect to the hold-downs after the wall is raised (**Figure 122**).

Where anchor posts attach to a corner stud or at one side of a wall opening, they must be located precisely. If possible, wire the anchor posts directly to the rebar. If the rebar is in the way, it

Figure 122. Hold-Down Installation

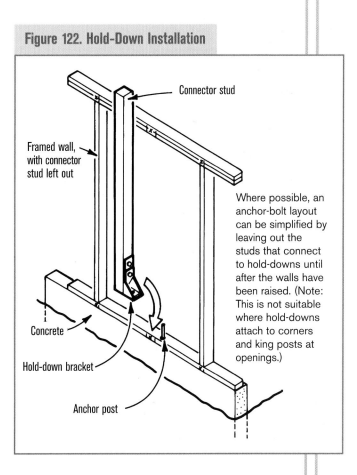

Connector stud

Framed wall, with connector stud left out

Where possible, an anchor-bolt layout can be simplified by leaving out the studs that connect to hold-downs until after the walls have been raised. (Note: This is not suitable where hold-downs attach to corners and king posts at openings.)

Concrete

Hold-down bracket

Anchor post

may be necessary to install the anchor posts slightly out of plumb (**Figure 123**).

Figure 123. Out-of-Plumb Anchor Bolts

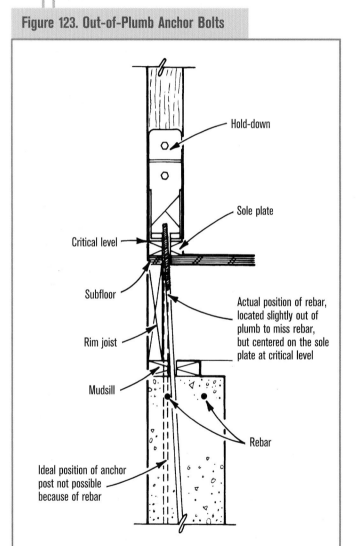

Hold-down

Sole plate

Critical level

Subfloor

Rim joist

Actual position of rebar, located slightly out of plumb to miss rebar, but centered on the sole plate at critical level

Mudsill

Rebar

Ideal position of anchor post not possible because of rebar

An anchor bolt may be slightly out of plumb if rebar is in the way. This will not affect the strength of the hold-down, but be sure the top end of the bolt is still centered where it comes through the sole plate.

Strap Anchors

These concrete-embedded metal straps nail or bolt to the face of the stud. Because they usually require no drilling, they are easier to install than hold-downs. However, they have significantly lower design loads. Also, the studs they nail to may split under the heavy nailing required. If so, replace the stud with a double stud or 4x member.

Stacked Wall Connections

There are several ways to reinforce the connection between floors (**Figure 124**). The most common approach for seismic work uses a pair of hold-downs with a large threaded rod between them. Other approaches use straps nailed directly to the studs or through the sheathing. In all cases, the studs must be aligned between floors. With metal straps, some builders use 4x4s because they are less prone to splitting with the large number of nails.

Roof Connections

Winds can exert strong uplift forces. Roofs with low slopes or large overhangs are more susceptible to these forces. Minimum code nailing schedules are rarely adequate to resist these forces.

Figure 124. Floor-to-Floor Connections

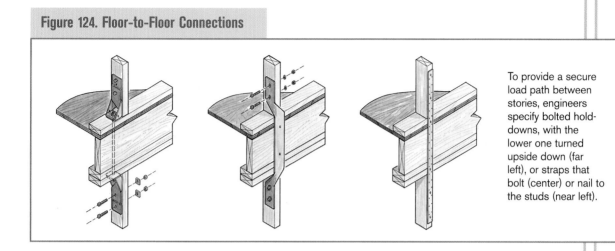

To provide a secure load path between stories, engineers specify bolted hold-downs, with the lower one turned upside down (far left), or straps that bolt (center) or nail to the studs (near left).

Adding wind ties, hurricane anchors, or other steel connectors at eaves connections is often required, and is good insurance in high-wind areas.

Framing Clips

A common detail in seismic zones is to connect the frieze block to the double top plate with a metal framing clip (**Figure 118**, exterior wall inset, page 75). These must be installed before the roof sheathing.

Hurricane Anchors

In high-wind areas, hurricane clips or rafter ties may be required to connect rafters or trusses to top plates (**Figure 125**). As with all rated connectors, the manufacturer's nailing schedule must be followed.

Figure 125. Eaves Connections

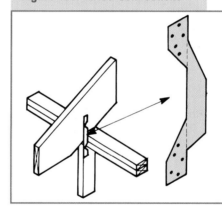

Nailing rafters to plates and plates to studs is not always enough to resist high winds. Some codes call for adequately rated hurricane anchors or rafter hold-downs at 4-ft. intervals in areas of high winds.

Ridge Connections

Steel connectors also may be required to reinforce the rafter connection at the ridge (**Figure 117**, page 74). These may consist of joist hangers installed at the ridge beam or rated steel straps placed across the tops of the opposing rafters. As with other strap connectors, nailing into 2x material may be a problem due to the number of fasteners.

Energy-Tight Details

Figure 126. Insulating the Rim Joist

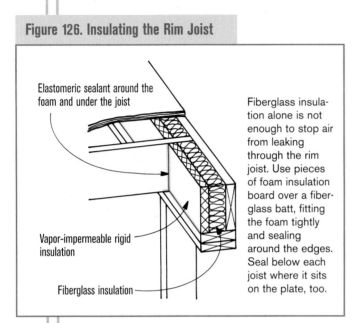

Elastomeric sealant around the foam and under the joist

Vapor-impermeable rigid insulation

Fiberglass insulation

Fiberglass insulation alone is not enough to stop air from leaking through the rim joist. Use pieces of foam insulation board over a fiberglass batt, fitting the foam tightly and sealing around the edges. Seal below each joist where it sits on the plate, too.

Figure 127. Offset Plates

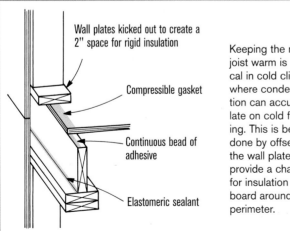

Wall plates kicked out to create a 2" space for rigid insulation

Compressible gasket

Continuous bead of adhesive

Elastomeric sealant

Keeping the rim joist warm is critical in cold climates where condensation can accumulate on cold framing. This is best done by offsetting the wall plates to provide a channel for insulation board around the perimeter.

Energy codes focus on air-sealing details, vapor barriers, and standard insulation values throughout the house. Good framing practice helps to ensure there is an adequate amount of insulation in all corners of the exterior shell. In addition, slight alterations in practice can make it easier to install a continuous air/vapor barrier on the inside of the house, as required by most energy codes in the U.S.

Sealing the Rim Joist

The rim joist is one of the greatest sources of air leaks in a wood-frame house. However, it is also one of the most difficult places to seal effectively.

The most common way to address this difficult area is to seal and insulate it after framing (**Figures 126**). Do not just stuff fiberglass into each joist bay. Foam insulation board, sealed tightly on all four sides, must be used to stop the flow of air and vapor.

When done thoroughly, fitting foam into each joist bay is time-consuming, so it's actually easier to address this area at the framing stage by offsetting the wall plates (**Figure 127**). This provides a 1¹/₂- to 2-in. cavity for strips of foam insulation board. Seal the corner between the rim joist and the bottom plate with urethane caulk and apply continuous beads of construction adhesive when installing floor sheathing and exterior walls.

Partition Channels

Interior partition channels in framed walls often create voids, which are inaccessible once the exterior walls are sheathed. **Figure 128** shows several ways wall channel can be detailed to provide an easily accessible insulation bay. To provide a continuous air/vapor barrier on the exterior walls, insulate and install a poly vapor barrier before standing the interior walls.

Sealing Knee Walls

The knee walls in a story-and-a-half Cape often create gaps in the insulation and/or in the air/vapor barrier. There are two common ways to insulate the knee wall area (both shown in **Figure 129**, page 82):

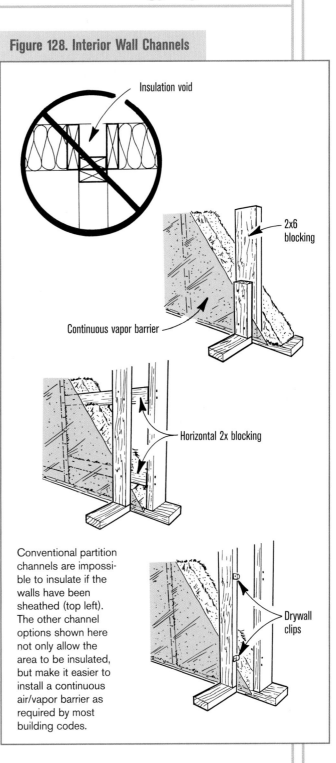

Figure 128. Interior Wall Channels

Insulation void

2x6 blocking

Continuous vapor barrier

Horizontal 2x blocking

Conventional partition channels are impossible to insulate if the walls have been sheathed (top left). The other channel options shown here not only allow the area to be insulated, but make it easier to install a continuous air/vapor barrier as required by most building codes.

Drywall clips

Follow the wall and floor. The more difficult way is to insulate the knee wall and the floor of the knee-wall area. Install a poly air/vapor over the insulation of the knee wall, as well as on the ceiling area below, taping it to an air block (foil-faced foam works well) between the joists just below the knee wall.

Follow the roof. An easier way to handle knee walls is to insulate the roof all the way down to the exterior wall — including a continuous vapor barrier on the inside face of the rafters — and then build the knee walls later. This works especially well if the knee-wall cavity will be used for storage. In this case, however, it's critical that the rim joist be sealed using foam board, as well.

Sealing Cantilevers

Many Colonial-style houses have a section of second floor cantilevered over the first-story wall. Without proper attention, this area can lose a lot of heat.

Keep track of the barrier. During construction, treat cantilevered floors like the floor-knee-wall transition, but install the vapor barrier on the subfloor of the second floor (**Figure 130**). Where the poly air barrier on the wall meets the floor, tape the plastic to the plywood. Then seal all the seams in the plywood subfloor with tape or caulk — that way, the plywood will function as an effective air barrier on the warm side of the insulation.

Block airflow at the floor. Between the cantilevered floor joists, fill the voids completely with fiberglass or cellulose insulation. Then install rigid foil-faced foam insulation in the bays

Figure 129. Knee Walls

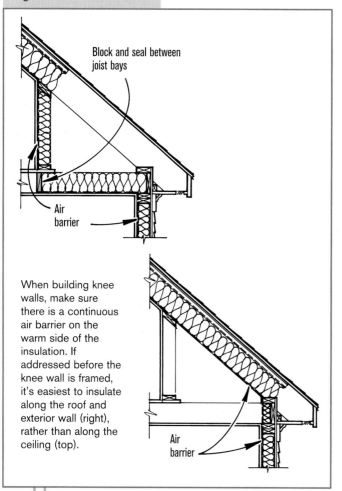

Block and seal between joist bays

Air barrier

When building knee walls, make sure there is a continuous air barrier on the warm side of the insulation. If addressed before the knee wall is framed, it's easiest to insulate along the roof and exterior wall (right), rather than along the ceiling (top).

Air barrier

where the joists bear on the first-floor wall and seal the edges where the foam meets the framing with caulk or foam. Tape the joint where the poly on the first-floor wall face meets the foam between the joists.

Sealing Balloon-Framed Walls

Gable-end walls and shed dormer front walls are often balloon-framed. In these situations, heated air enters the wall through a penetration — such as an electrical outlet or even a crack around the baseboard and drywall at the bottom of the wall. The warm air rises in the stud cavity like smoke in a chimney, escaping into the cold attic and exiting through the roof vents. But even where there is no penetration in the wall, cold air from the attic will drop into the stud cavity where it is warmed by the wall and rises back into the attic. This kind of *convection loop* carries heat out of the house.

To prevent this type of heat loss, install wall blocking in line with the ceiling joists (**Figure 131**).

Sealing Framing Projections

Eyebrow roofs, bay window roofs, crickets, and other projections of the wall or roof lines are sometimes built

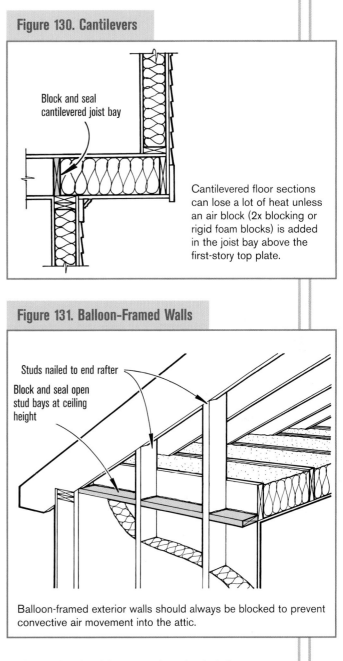

Figure 130. Cantilevers

Block and seal cantilevered joist bay

Cantilevered floor sections can lose a lot of heat unless an air block (2x blocking or rigid foam blocks) is added in the joist bay above the first-story top plate.

Figure 131. Balloon-Framed Walls

Studs nailed to end rafter

Block and seal open stud bays at ceiling height

Balloon-framed exterior walls should always be blocked to prevent convective air movement into the attic.

before the building is sheathed. This allows air to penetrate the exterior walls and leak out the building.

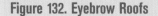

Figure 132. Eyebrow Roofs

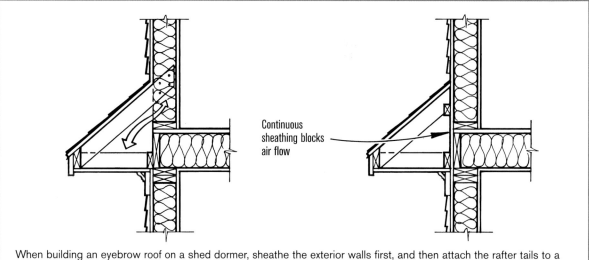

Continuous
sheathing blocks
air flow

When building an eyebrow roof on a shed dormer, sheathe the exterior walls first, and then attach the rafter tails to a ledger (right).

To avoid these heat losses, always sheathe the exterior walls and then attach additional framing to a ledger (**Figure 132**).

Cathedral Ceiling Options

Cathedral ceilings must have adequate insulation (R-38 to R-40 in cold climates) and ventilation, but it can be a challenge to provide both in the space provided by a typical 12-in. rafter.

Hot vs. Cold Roofs

Most codes require new roofs to have an eaves-to-ridge flow of air. These are called *cold roofs* because they keep the underside of the sheathing cold in winter. In a heating climate, the flow of cold air under the sheathing discourages interior moisture buildup and ice damming. In a cooling climate, ventilation relieves heat buildup.

Cathedral ceilings that aren't ventilated are referred to as *hot roofs*, and typically rely on a well-sealed air and vapor barrier to keep moisture out of the roof. Solid-foam roof systems, using stress-skin panels or spray-in foam, are hot roof alternatives. However, many code officials do not permit these roofs. The cathedral ceiling options shown in this manual are all cold-roof options.

Figure 133. Cathedral Ceiling Options

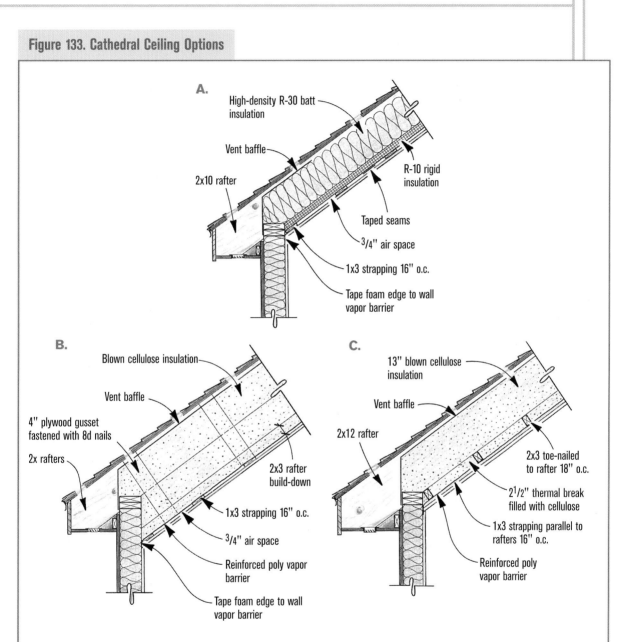

A.
High-density R-30 batt insulation
Vent baffle
2x10 rafter
R-10 rigid insulation
Taped seams
3/4" air space
1x3 strapping 16" o.c.
Tape foam edge to wall vapor barrier

B.
Blown cellulose insulation
Vent baffle
4" plywood gusset fastened with 8d nails
2x rafters
2x3 rafter build-down
1x3 strapping 16" o.c.
3/4" air space
Reinforced poly vapor barrier
Tape foam edge to wall vapor barrier

C.
13" blown cellulose insulation
Vent baffle
2x12 rafter
2x3 toe-nailed to rafter 18" o.c.
2 1/2" thermal break filled with cellulose
1x3 strapping parallel to rafters 16" o.c.
Reinforced poly vapor barrier

A. Foil-faced foam sheets applied to the bottom of 2x rafters boost the ceiling's R-value and provide a thermal break. Tape the seams between the foam sheets to reduce air and vapor movement into the ceiling cavity.
B. Hang 2x3s below rafters using plywood gussets to create as wide a space as needed for blown cellulose insulation.
C. Insulation space can be added by installing 2x3s toenailed across the bottom edge of the rafters, which also provides a thermal break.

Figure 133. Cathedral Ceiling Options, continued

D.

Scissor truss with 12" raised heel

Minimum 2" air space

Wind baffle (extend sheathing)

Vent to continuous ridge vent

Continuous soffit vent

1¹/2" air space

12" fiberglass batts

2x3 furring

Continuous poly vapor barrier

E.

Blown cellulose insulation

Vent channel

16" deep wood I-joist

1x3 strapping 16" o.c.

³/4" air space

Reinforced poly vapor barrier

Tape seams of vapor barrier

F.

Ridge vent at top

Sheathing

1" air space to ridge vent

Cardboard vent baffles

Soffit vent

10¹/4" min. blown-in fiberglass

⁵/8" drywall with vapor barrier paint

2x12s 24" on-center (shaded)

2x6 open rafter tails

D. Scissors trusses with raised heels provide adequate space for insulation. Batts must be carefully fitted to minimize short-circuiting at truss chords.

E. 16-in.-deep I-joists insulated with dense-blown cellulose.

F. High R-value insulation (blown-in fiberglass) can be substituted for standard fiberglass batts or blown-in cellulose.

Cathedral Framing Options

Cathedral roofs framed with conventional 2x10 or 2x12 rafters typically do not provide adequate space for insulation in cold climates. The rafters need to be packed out to provide more space or foam insulation should be added to the underside (**Figure 133**, pages 85-86).

Thermal break. Since wood is not very good insulation, the rafters themselves conduct cold through the roof. Most of the framing options shown in **Figure 133** provide a *thermal break*: an interruption of the conducting material (in this case, wood) intended to reduce continuous heat flow through the rafter.

Insulation options. The R-values of insulation materials vary widely, as shown in **Figure 134**, so installing insulation with a higher R-value may be the easiest alternative for cathedral ceilings. For example, high-performance batts or blown-in fiberglass (BIBS) can be used to bring the R-value of a 2x12 rafter space to an acceptable R-38 to R-40 (**Figure 133**, option F).

Vent baffle. In every cold-roof option shown in **Figure 133**, a vent baffle (using cardboard or vent channel)

must be installed to provide uninterrupted airflow from eaves vents to a ridge vent.

Alternative Framing Options

An alternative to conventional rafters is to use scissors trusses or deep I-joists — these provide enough space for the extra insulation needed to achieve a higher R-value (**Figure 133**, options D and E).

Figure 134. Insulation R-Values

Insulation	Approx. R-Value per in.
Fiberglass batt	3.2
High-performance fiberglass batt	3.8
Loose-fill fiberglass	2.5
Blown-in fiberglass (BIBS)	4
Loose-fill cellulose	3.5
Dense-pack cellulose	3.5
Perlite or vermiculite	2.7
Expanded polystyrene board	3.8
Extruded polystyrene board	4.8
Foil-faced polyisocyanurate board	7
Spray-urethane foam	5.9

Steel in Wood Frames

Because of the high bearing capacity of steel, it is a useful alternative for carrying heavy loads, particularly where space is limited. **Figure 135** shows the types of steel that can be useful for columns, beams, and brackets in wood-framed construction.

Figure 135. Steel Types and Sizes

	Shape & Type	Symbol	Stock Size Specs	Lengths	Finish	Uses
I-Beams I	Junior[1]	M	Height in inches	20, 40,	Hot-rolled,	Carrying beams,
	Standard	S	x pounds/LF	50, and	mill finish	headers, ridge beams,
	Wide Flange	W or WF	(Ex: W8x24)	60 feet		cantilevered beams
Channels [	Stringer[1]	MC	Height in inches	20 and	Hot-rolled,	Carrying beams,
	Standard	C	x pounds/LF)	40 feet	mill finish	flitchplates, headers,
	Ship & Car[2]	MC	(Ex: C5x9			ridge beams, columns
Tee T	Tee[3]	T	Height in inches x width in inches (Ex: T6x8)	20 feet	Hot-rolled, mill finish	Lintels, ledgers, light-load columns
Angles L L	Equal Legs Unequal Legs	Angle in degrees or L	Leg x leg x thickness (Ex: 3x6x1/4")	20 and 40 feet	Hot-rolled, mill finish	Lintels, ledgers, web and flange reinforcements joint clips
Bar Stock — ● ■	Flats Rounds Squares	N/A	Thickness x width (Ex: 1/2x8) Diameter (Ex: 2") Width of one side (Ex: 1")	20 feet, 12 feet and random	Hot-rolled, mill finish Cold-rolled, pickled and oiled	Column plates, splice plates, machinist parts, tools
Pipe ○	Sch. 10[1] Sch. 40 Sch. 80[2]	BPPE (black pipe plain end)or BPTC (black pipe threaded coupling)	Inside diameter x schedule weight (3" Sch. 40 BPPE)	21 to 24 feet	Hot-rolled, mill finish, painted, hot galv.	Columns
Tubing ○ □ ▭	Round Square Rectangular	ERW (elec.-res. welded) DOM (drawn over mandrel)	Outside dim. or diameter x wall thickness (Ex: 2x^1/8" round; 2x4x^1/4" rectangle)	20 and 40 feet	Hot- or cold-rolled, pickled and oiled	Handrails, balusters, specialties

(1) Also called "Lightweight"   (2) Also called "Heavyweight"   (3) Made by splitting I-beams in half

Each grade of structural steel has a specific quality as described by American Society of Testing and Materials (ASTM) standards. ASTM A-326 is the predominant grade in the structural steel market. It has a carbon content of .26%, which gives it relatively high strength (60,000 psi tensile), yet it is relatively easy to weld and fabricate.

Structural Steel Headers

Where height is limited, but a header must be installed to carry a heavy point load (a second-floor girder resting on a sliding-glass door header, for example), steel is often the only solution. **Figure 136** shows examples of standard steel shapes and sizes that will work as headers to carry such heavy point loads. Each of these pieces of steel can be worked into a 2x4 wall, although the W beams (commonly called I-beams) are a full 4 in. wide and require careful work to fit.

Figure 136. Structural Steel Headers

Point Load (lb.)	Span 3'	4'	5'	6'
5,000	T3x3x^5/16	T4x4x^3/16	T4x3x^1/4	C6x8.2
	(1.88)	(2.50)	(3.13)	(3.75)
10,000	C6x8.2	C6x10.5	W6x12	T6x3x^3/8
	(3.75)	(5.00)	(6.25)	(7.50)
15,000	C6x13	T6x3x^3/8	T7x3x^3/8	W8x15
	(5.63)	(7.50)	(9.38)	(11.25)
20,000	T6x3x^3/8	W6x16	W10x15	W10x17
	(7.50)	(10.00)	(13.00)	(15.00)

T   C   W

The number in parentheses is the section modulus required for the given load and span; the steel section above it is the shallowest and lightest piece of steel that will work. Substitutions may have to be made because the steel yard may not carry every size and shape.

Figure 137. Splicing I-Beams

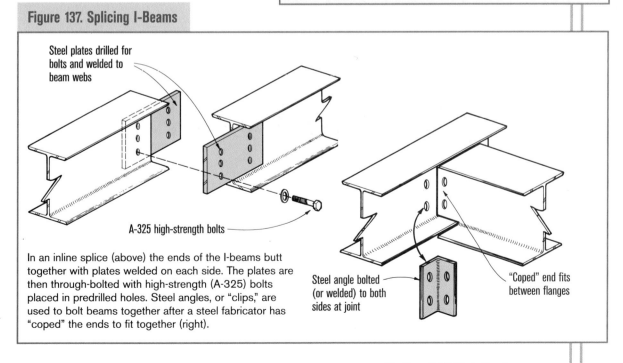

Steel plates drilled for bolts and welded to beam webs

A-325 high-strength bolts

Steel angle bolted (or welded) to both sides at joint

"Coped" end fits between flanges

In an inline splice (above) the ends of the I-beams butt together with plates welded on each side. The plates are then through-bolted with high-strength (A-325) bolts placed in predrilled holes. Steel angles, or "clips," are used to bolt beams together after a steel fabricator has "coped" the ends to fit together (right).

Figure 138. Column Connections

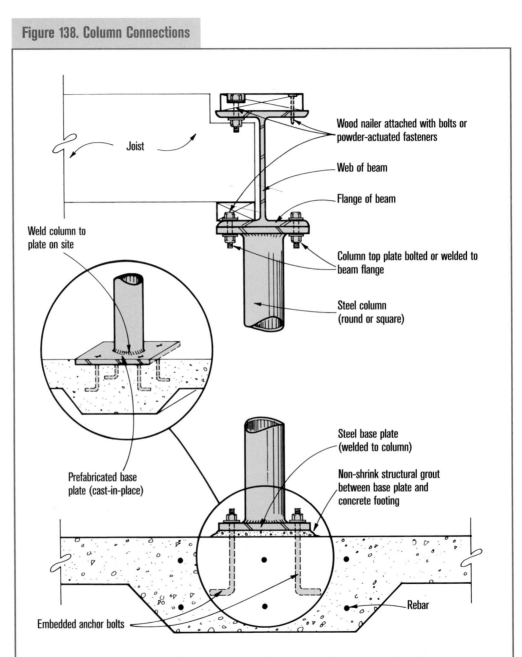

Joist

Wood nailer attached with bolts or powder-actuated fasteners

Web of beam

Flange of beam

Weld column to plate on site

Column top plate bolted or welded to beam flange

Steel column (round or square)

Prefabricated base plate (cast-in-place)

Steel base plate (welded to column)

Non-shrink structural grout between base plate and concrete footing

Rebar

Embedded anchor bolts

Steel columns (not wood posts) should be used when freestanding support of steel beams is required. The column plates must be bolted to beam flanges (top) and to the thickened slab footing (bottom). An alternative is to weld column plates to beam flanges, and weld column bases to steel base plates cast into the slab footings (inset).

Jack Support

Headers should be supported by at least double 2x4 jack studs for up to a 12,000-lb. load and triple jacks for loads above 12,000 lb. up to 18,000 lb. The header should sit directly on the end grain of the jack studs. Don't use wood shims under the header — the load is perpendicular to the grain and tends to crush the wood.

Steel-to-Steel Connections

Most steel connections are either bolted or welded together. Welding is useful when the surface area to be joined is small, such as the edge of a steel column.

Bolted connections, on the other hand, don't require special skills. The most common bolted connections are in-line splices and beam-to-beam connections at right angles (**Figure 137**, page 89), and where column plates join footings and beam flanges (**Figure 138**).

Right-angle connections (**Figure 137**, page 89) require the flange of one beam to be cut back ("coped") at one end so that the webs of each beam fit together. It doesn't have to be perfect, since the bolts will carry the load.

For any bolted structural connection, an engineer should specify the diameter and length of the bolts needed for the type of connection. These will probably be high-strength, structural steel (A-325) bolts, which are available from steel supply houses or steelwork shops.

Steel-to-Concrete Connections

Column bases must be bolted into concrete. Don't count on concrete alone to hold embedded steel in place. The concrete will shrink away over time, so you should attach the steel to anchor bolts. When embedding steel base plate for column supports, attach hooks to a portion of the steel that will be surrounded by concrete (inset, **Figure 138**). These will "grab" and prevent movement of the steel once the concrete has shrunk.

Steel-to-Wood Connections

There are several ways to attach steel to wood, depending on the circumstances. **Figure 139**, page 92 shows some common steel-to-wood connections using different steel shapes.

Nailers

Wood nailers are easiest to attach with powder-actuated nails, spaced 24- to 36-in. o.c. and staggered side-to-side.

Figure 139. Steel-to-Wood Connections

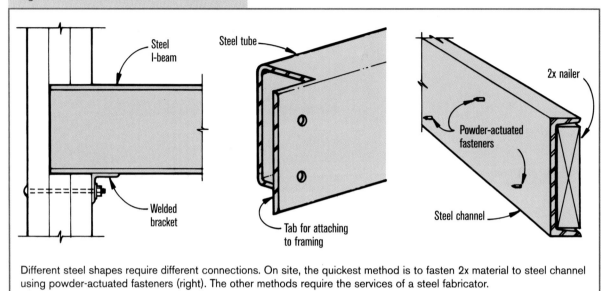

Steel I-beam

Steel tube

2x nailer

Powder-actuated fasteners

Welded bracket

Tab for attaching to framing

Steel channel

Different steel shapes require different connections. On site, the quickest method is to fasten 2x material to steel channel using powder-actuated fasteners (right). The other methods require the services of a steel fabricator.

Figure 140. Steel Header Connection

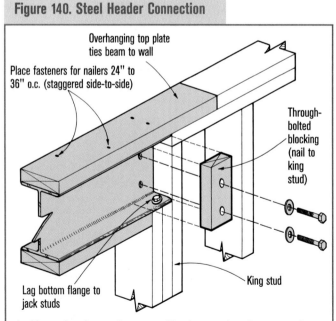

Overhanging top plate ties beam to wall

Place fasteners for nailers 24" to 36" o.c. (staggered side-to-side)

Through-bolted blocking (nail to king stud)

Lag bottom flange to jack studs

King stud

An I-beam header can be secured by the top plate that spans the connection between the beam and the wall. This connection should be reinforced with lag bolts into the bottom flange to the jack studs, and with bolt-on blocking that is toe-nailed to the king stud.

Header Connections

A common way to attach an I-beam header to wood framing is to have the steel yard weld on an angle bracket, as shown in the left-hand illustration of **Figure 139**. An alternative is to secure the connection using a top plate, which overlaps the steel and wood-framed walls (**Figure 140**).

For slim-profile tube headers where there is not enough room to "nail on" lumber (using a powder-actuated tool), ask the steel fabricator to leave a tab sticking out at each end, as shown in the center illustration of **Figure 139**. Then notch the framing to fit, and nail or lag the steel to the framing.

Flitchplates

Flitchplates are used primarily in header assemblies when common framing lumber is not strong enough or stiff enough to carry the loads (**Figure 141**).

The steel is put in the middle for two reasons. First, this increases fire resistance. Wood can resist fire longer than steel, which softens very quickly in a fire. Second, the steel is not likely to buckle if placed between two wood members. A thin plate of steel will wrinkle and buckle under relatively small loads unless stabilized.

End Connections

An engineer should specify the size and number of bolts required to secure a flitch plate to the wood framing. Insufficient bolting and poorly sized bolt-holes will cause the wood around the bolts to crush and the plates to settle. In extreme cases, the steel can knife into the top of the post.

As a rule of thumb, bolt-holes should be placed 2 in. from all edges of a beam. Use the flitchplate as a template to precisely align the holes in the wood.

Figure 141. Equivalent Strengths: Flitch Beams vs. Built-Up Wood Beams & Steel I-Beams

Wood	Single Steel Flitch Beam / Steel	Built-Up Lumber Equivalents*	Steel I-Beam Equivalents	Wood	Double Steel Flitch Beam / Steel	Built-Up Lumber Equivalents*	Steel I-Beam Equivalents
2x6	5" x $^1/_4$"	2.3 - 2x6s	–	2x6	5" x $^1/_4$"	4.7 - 2x6s	–
	5 x $^3/_8$	3.5 - 2x6s	–		5 x $^3/_8$	7 - 2x6s	–
	5 x $^1/_2$	4.7 - 2x6s	–		5 x $^1/_2$	9.4 - 2x6s	–
2x8	7 x $^1/_4$	2.8 - 2x8s	–	2x8	7 x $^1/_4$	5.6 - 2x8s	W6x9
	7 x $^3/_8$	4.2 - 2x8s	–		7 x $^3/_8$	8.4 - 2x8s	W8x10 or W6x12
	7 x $^1/_2$	5.6 - 2x8s	W6x9		7 x $^1/_2$	11.3 - 2x8s	W8x13
2x10	9 x $^1/_4$	2.9 - 2x10s	–	2x10	9 x $^1/_4$	5.6 - 2x10s	W8x10
	9 x $^3/_8$	4.3 - 2x10s	–		9 x $^3/_8$	8.4 - 2x10s	W8x15
	9 x $^1/_2$	5.8 - 2x10s	W8x10		9 x $^1/_2$	11.5 - 2x10s	W8x18
2x12	11 x $^1/_4$	2.9 - 2x12s	–	2x12	11 x $^1/_4$	5.8 - 2x12s	W10x12
	11 x $^3/_8$	4.4 - 2x12s	–		11 x $^3/_8$	8.8 - 2x12s	W10x17
	11 x $^1/_2$	5.8 - 2x12s	W10x12		11 x $^1/_2$	11.7 - 2x12s	W10x22

* The strength equivalent shown for built-up lumber beams assumes Doug-fir-larch (E = 1.6, Fb = 1,200).

Figure 24. Maximum Allowable Spans (ft.-in.) for Floor Joists

Residential Living Areas: 40 PSF Live, 10 PSF Dead (L/360)

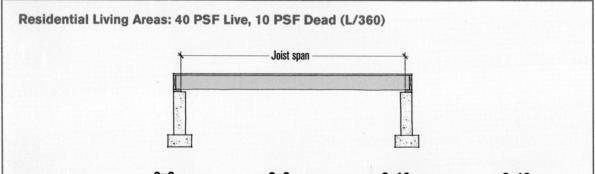

Species Group	Spacing (in.)	2x6 No. 1	2x6 No. 2	2x6 No. 1-2 (Can.)	2x8 No. 1	2x8 No. 2	2x8 No. 1-2 (Can.)	2x10 No. 1	2x10 No. 2	2x10 No. 1-2 (Can.)	2x12 No. 1	2x12 No. 2	2x12 No. 1-2 (Can.)
D-Fir-L	12	10-11	10-9	10-9	14-5	14-2	14-2	18-5	18-0	17-6	22-0	20-11	20-4
	16	9-11	9-9	9-9	13-1	12-9	12-5	16-5	15-7	15-2	19-1	18-1	17-7
	24	8-8	8-3	8-0	11-0	10-5	10-2	13-5	12-9	12-5	15-7	14-9	14-4
SPF	12	–	–	10-3	–	–	13-6	–	–	17-3	–	–	20-7
	16	–	–	9-4	–	–	12-3	–	–	15-5	–	–	17-10
	24	–	–	8-1	–	–	10-3	–	–	12-7	–	–	14-7
Hem-Fir	12	10-6	10-0	10-9	13-10	13-2	14-2	17-8	16-10	18-0	21-6	20-4	21-11
	16	9-6	9-1	9-9	12-7	12-0	12-10	16-0	15-2	16-5	18-10	17-7	19-1
	24	8-4	7-11	8-6	10-10	10-2	11-0	13-3	12-5	13-5	15-5	14-4	15-7
SYP	12	10-11	10-9	–	14-5	14-2	–	18-5	18-0	–	22-5	21-9	–
	16	9-11	9-9	–	13-1	12-10	–	16-9	16-1	–	20-4	18-10	–
	24	8-8	8-6	–	11-5	11-0	–	14-7	13-2	–	17-5	15-4	–

For information on framing joists, see pages 22-30.

Figure 25. Maximum Allowable Spans (ft.-in.) for Floor Joists

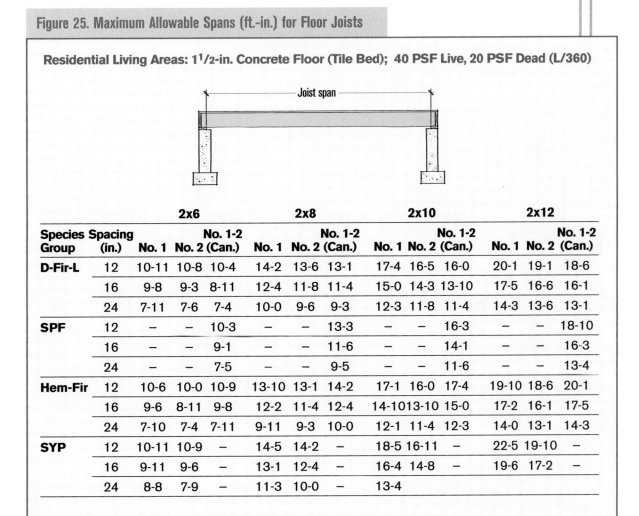

Residential Living Areas: 1$^1/_2$-in. Concrete Floor (Tile Bed); 40 PSF Live, 20 PSF Dead (L/360)

Species Group	Spacing (in.)	2x6 No. 1	2x6 No. 2	2x6 No. 1-2 (Can.)	2x8 No. 1	2x8 No. 2	2x8 No. 1-2 (Can.)	2x10 No. 1	2x10 No. 2	2x10 No. 1-2 (Can.)	2x12 No. 1	2x12 No. 2	2x12 No. 1-2 (Can.)
D-Fir-L	12	10-11	10-8	10-4	14-2	13-6	13-1	17-4	16-5	16-0	20-1	19-1	18-6
	16	9-8	9-3	8-11	12-4	11-8	11-4	15-0	14-3	13-10	17-5	16-6	16-1
	24	7-11	7-6	7-4	10-0	9-6	9-3	12-3	11-8	11-4	14-3	13-6	13-1
SPF	12	–	–	10-3	–	–	13-3	–	–	16-3	–	–	18-10
	16	–	–	9-1	–	–	11-6	–	–	14-1	–	–	16-3
	24	–	–	7-5	–	–	9-5	–	–	11-6	–	–	13-4
Hem-Fir	12	10-6	10-0	10-9	13-10	13-1	14-2	17-1	16-0	17-4	19-10	18-6	20-1
	16	9-6	8-11	9-8	12-2	11-4	12-4	14-10	13-10	15-0	17-2	16-1	17-5
	24	7-10	7-4	7-11	9-11	9-3	10-0	12-1	11-4	12-3	14-0	13-1	14-3
SYP	12	10-11	10-9	–	14-5	14-2	–	18-5	16-11	–	22-5	19-10	–
	16	9-11	9-6	–	13-1	12-4	–	16-4	14-8	–	19-6	17-2	–
	24	8-8	7-9	–	11-3	10-0	–	13-4					

For information on framing joists, see pages 22-30.

Figure 26. Maximum Allowable Spans (ft.-in.) for Ceiling Joists

Drywall Attached – No Future Rooms and No Attic Storage; 10 PSF Live 5 PSF Dead (L/240)

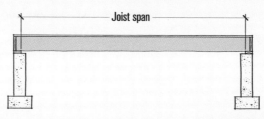

Species Group	Spacing (in.)	2x4 No. 1	2x4 No. 2	2x4 No. 1-2 (Can.)	2x6 No. 1	2x6 No. 2	2x6 No. 1-2 (Can.)	2x8 No. 1	2x8 No. 2	2x8 No. 1-2 (Can.)	2x10 No. 1	2x10 No. 2	2x10 No. 1-2 (Can.)
D-Fir-L	12	12-8	12-5	12-5	19-11	19-6	19-6	26-2	25-8	25-8	33-5	32-9	32-0
	16	11-6	11-3	11-3	18-1	17-8	17-8	23-10	23-4	22-8	30-0	28-6	27-8
	24	10-0	9-10	9-10	15-9	15-0	14-7	20-1	19-1	18-6	24-6	23-3	22-7
SPF	12	–	–	11-10	–	–	18-8	–	–	24-7	–	–	31-4
	16	–	–	10-9	–	–	16-11	–	–	22-4	–	–	28-1
	24	–	–	9-5	–	–	14-9	–	–	18-9	–	–	22-11
Hem-Fir	12	12-2	11-7	12-5	19-1	18-2	19-6	25-2	24-0	25-8	32-1	30-7	32-9
	16	11-0	10-6	11-3	17-4	16-6	17-8	22-10	21-9	23-4	29-2	27-8	29-9
	24	9-8	9-2	9-10	15-2	14-5	15-6	19-10	18-6	20-1	24-3	22-7	24-6
SYP	12	12-8	12-5	–	19-11	19-6	–	26-2	25-8	–	33-5	32-9	–
	16	11-6	11-3	–	18-1	17-8	–	23-10	23-4	–	30-5	29-4	–
	24	10-0	9-10	–	15-9	15-6	–	20-10	20-1	–	26-6	24-0	–

For information on framing joists, see pages 22-30.

Figure 27. Maximum Allowable Spans (ft.-in.) for Ceiling Joists

Drywall Attached – No Future Rooms, Limited Attic Storage; 20 PSF Live 10 PSF Dead (L/240)

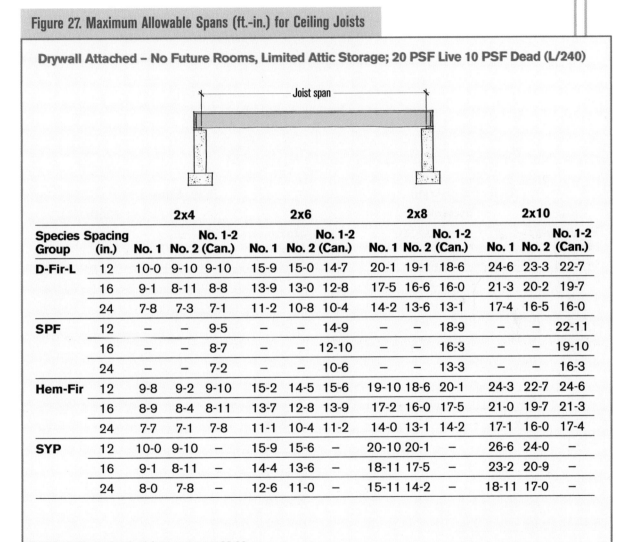

Species Group	Spacing (in.)	2x4 No. 1	2x4 No. 2	2x4 No. 1-2 (Can.)	2x6 No. 1	2x6 No. 2	2x6 No. 1-2 (Can.)	2x8 No. 1	2x8 No. 2	2x8 No. 1-2 (Can.)	2x10 No. 1	2x10 No. 2	2x10 No. 1-2 (Can.)
D-Fir-L	12	10-0	9-10	9-10	15-9	15-0	14-7	20-1	19-1	18-6	24-6	23-3	22-7
	16	9-1	8-11	8-8	13-9	13-0	12-8	17-5	16-6	16-0	21-3	20-2	19-7
	24	7-8	7-3	7-1	11-2	10-8	10-4	14-2	13-6	13-1	17-4	16-5	16-0
SPF	12	–	–	9-5	–	–	14-9	–	–	18-9	–	–	22-11
	16	–	–	8-7	–	–	12-10	–	–	16-3	–	–	19-10
	24	–	–	7-2	–	–	10-6	–	–	13-3	–	–	16-3
Hem-Fir	12	9-8	9-2	9-10	15-2	14-5	15-6	19-10	18-6	20-1	24-3	22-7	24-6
	16	8-9	8-4	8-11	13-7	12-8	13-9	17-2	16-0	17-5	21-0	19-7	21-3
	24	7-7	7-1	7-8	11-1	10-4	11-2	14-0	13-1	14-2	17-1	16-0	17-4
SYP	12	10-0	9-10	–	15-9	15-6	–	20-10	20-1	–	26-6	24-0	–
	16	9-1	8-11	–	14-4	13-6	–	18-11	17-5	–	23-2	20-9	–
	24	8-0	7-8	–	12-6	11-0	–	15-11	14-2	–	18-11	17-0	–

For information on framing joists, see pages 22-30.

Figure 60. Header and Girder Spans (ft.-in.) for Exterior Bearing Walls

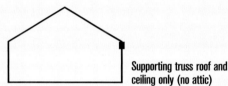

Supporting truss roof and
ceiling only (no attic)

20 lb. Snow Load
Building Width (ft.)

Maximum Header Size	20		36	
	Span	No. of Jacks	Span	No. of Jacks
2-2x4	3-6	1	2-10	1
2-2x6	5-5	1	4-2	1
2-2x8	6-10	1	5-4	2
2-2x10	8-5	2	6-6	2
2-2x12	9-9	2	7-6	2
3-2x8	8-4	1	6-8	1
3-2x10	10-6	1	8-2	2
3-2x12	12-2	2	9-5	2
4-2x8	9-2	1	7-8	2
4-2x10	11-8	1	9-5	2
4-2x12	14-1	1	10-11	2

50 lb. Snow Load
Building Width (ft.)

Maximum Header Size	20		36	
	Span	No. of Jacks	Span	No. of Jacks
2-2x4	2-10	1	2-2	1
2-2x6	4-1	1	3-2	2
2-2x8	5-2	2	4-0	2
2-2x10	6-4	2	4-11	2
2-2x12	7-4	2	5-8	3
3-2x8	6-6	2	5-0	2
3-2x10	7-11	2	6-2	2
3-2x12	9-2	2	7-2	2
4-2x8	7-6	2	5-10	2
4-2x10	9-2	2	7-1	2
4-2x12	10-8	2	8-3	2

Note: Calculated spans assume #2 grade Doug.-Fir, Hem-Fir and SYP lumber.

Figure 61. Header and Girder Spans (ft.-in.) for Exterior Bearing Walls

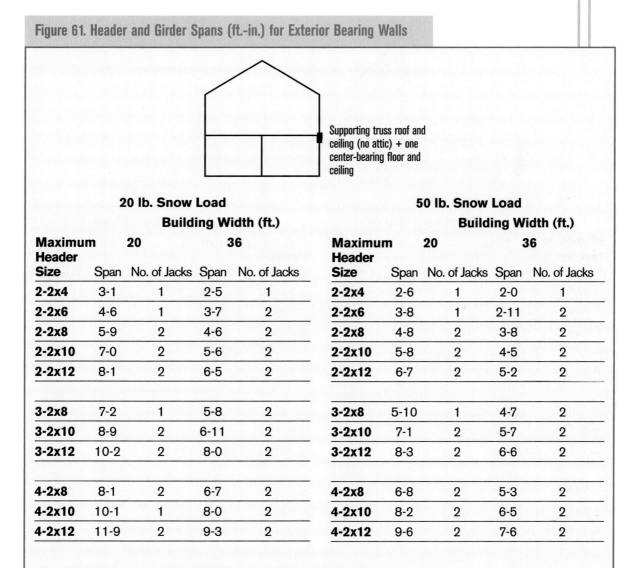

Supporting truss roof and ceiling (no attic) + one center-bearing floor and ceiling

20 lb. Snow Load
Building Width (ft.)

Maximum Header Size	20 Span	No. of Jacks	36 Span	No. of Jacks
2-2x4	3-1	1	2-5	1
2-2x6	4-6	1	3-7	2
2-2x8	5-9	2	4-6	2
2-2x10	7-0	2	5-6	2
2-2x12	8-1	2	6-5	2
3-2x8	7-2	1	5-8	2
3-2x10	8-9	2	6-11	2
3-2x12	10-2	2	8-0	2
4-2x8	8-1	2	6-7	2
4-2x10	10-1	1	8-0	2
4-2x12	11-9	2	9-3	2

50 lb. Snow Load
Building Width (ft.)

Maximum Header Size	20 Span	No. of Jacks	36 Span	No. of Jacks
2-2x4	2-6	1	2-0	1
2-2x6	3-8	1	2-11	2
2-2x8	4-8	2	3-8	2
2-2x10	5-8	2	4-5	2
2-2x12	6-7	2	5-2	2
3-2x8	5-10	1	4-7	2
3-2x10	7-1	2	5-7	2
3-2x12	8-3	2	6-6	2
4-2x8	6-8	2	5-3	2
4-2x10	8-2	2	6-5	2
4-2x12	9-6	2	7-6	2

Note: Calculated spans assume #2 grade Doug.-Fir, Hem-Fir and SYP lumber.

Figure 62. Header and Girder Spans (ft.-in.) for Exterior Bearing Walls

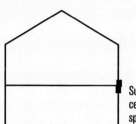

Supporting truss roof and ceiling (no attic) + clear-span floor and ceiling

	20 lb. Snow Load					50 lb. Snow Load			
	Building Width (ft.)					Building Width (ft.)			
Maximum Header Size	20		36		Maximum Header Size	20		36	
	Span	No. of Jacks	Span	No. of Jacks		Span	No. of Jacks	Span	No. of Jacks
2-2x4	2-8	1	2-1	1	2-2x4	2-5	1	1-10	1
2-2x6	3-11	1	3-0	2	2-2x6	3-6	2	2-9	2
2-2x8	5-0	2	3-10	2	2-2x8	4-5	2	3-5	2
2-2x10	6-1	2	4-8	2	2-2x10	5-5	2	4-3	3
2-2x12	7-1	2	5-5	3	2-2x12	6-3	2	4-11	3
3-2x8	6-3	2	4-10	2	3-2x8	5-6	2	4-4	2
3-2x10	7-7	2	5-11	2	3-2x10	6-9	2	5-3	2
3-2x12	8-10	2	6-10	2	3-2x12	7-10	2	6-1	2
4-2x8	7-2	2	5-7	2	4-2x8	6-4	2	5-0	2
4-2x10	8-9	2	6-10	2	4-2x10	7-9	2	6-1	2
4-2x12	10-2	2	7-11	2	4-2x12	9-0	2	7-1	2

Note: Calculated spans assume #2 grade Doug.-Fir, Hem-Fir and SYP lumber.

Figure 63. Header and Girder Spans (ft.-in.) for Exterior Bearing Walls

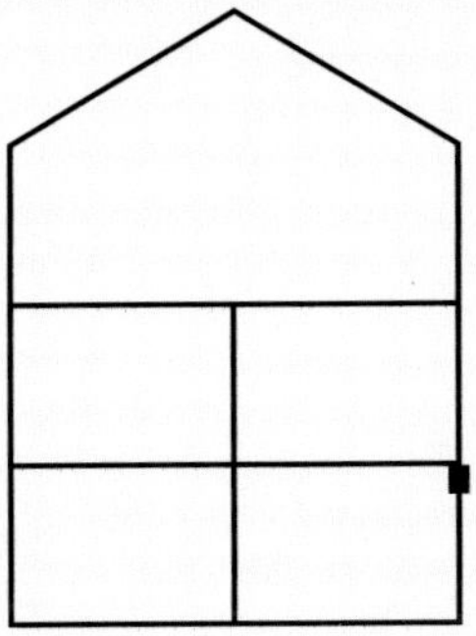

Supporting truss roof and ceiling (no attic) + two center-bearing floors and ceilings

	20 lb. Snow Load				50 lb. Snow Load			
	Building Width (ft.)				Building Width (ft.)			
Maximum Header Size	20		36		Maximum Header Size	20		36	
	Span	No. of Jacks	Span	No. of Jacks		Span	No. of Jacks	Span	No. of Jacks
2-2x4	2-7	1	2-0	1	2-2x4	2-3	1	1-10	1
2-2x6	3-9	2	2-11	2	2-2x6	3-4	2	2-8	2
2-2x8	4-9	2	3-9	2	2-2x8	4-3	2	3-4	2
2-2x10	5-9	2	4-7	3	2-2x10	5-2	2	4-1	3
2-2x12	6-8	2	5-3	3	2-2x12	6-0	2	4-9	3
3-2x8	5-11	2	4-8	2	3-2x8	5-4	2	4-2	2
3-2x10	7-3	2	5-9	2	3-2x10	6-6	2	5-2	2
3-2x12	8-5	2	6-7	2	3-2x12	7-6	2	6-0	3
4-2x8	6-10	2	5-5	2	4-2x8	6-1	2	4-10	2
4-2x10	8-4	2	6-7	2	4-2x10	7-6	2	5-11	2
4-2x12	9-8	2	7-8	2	4-2x12	8-8	2	6-11	2

Note: Calculated spans assume #2 grade Doug.-Fir, Hem-Fir and SYP lumber.

Figure 64. Header and Girder Spans (ft.-in.) for Exterior Bearing Walls

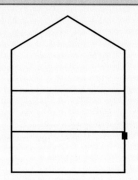

Supporting truss roof and ceiling (no attic) + two clear-span floors and ceilings

20 lb. Snow Load
Building Width (ft.)

Maximum Header Size	20		36	
	Span	No. of Jacks	Span	No. of Jacks
2-2x4	2-1	1	1-7	2
2-2x6	3-1	2	2-4	2
2-2x8	3-10	2	3-0	3
2-2x10	4-9	2	3-8	3
2-2x12	5-6	3	4-3	3
3-2x8	4-10	2	3-9	2
3-2x10	5-11	2	4-7	3
3-2x12	6-10	2	5-4	3
4-2x8	5-7	2	4-4	3
4-2x10	6-10	2	5-3	2
4-2x12	7-11	2	6-2	3

50 lb. Snow Load
Building Width (ft.)

Maximum Header Size	20		36	
	Span	No. of Jacks	Span	No. of Jacks
2-2x4	2-0	1	1-7	2
2-2x6	2-11	2	2-3	2
2-2x8	3-9	2	2-11	3
2-2x10	4-7	2	3-6	3
2-2x12	5-3	3	4-1	3
3-2x8	4-8	2	3-7	2
3-2x10	5-8	2	4-5	3
3-2x12	6-7	2	5-1	3
4-2x8	5-5	2	4-2	3
4-2x10	6-7	2	5-1	2
4-2x12	7-8	2	5-11	3

Note: Calculated spans assume #2 grade Doug.-Fir, Hem-Fir and SYP lumber.

Figure 65. Header and Girder Spans (ft.-in.) for Interior Bearing Walls

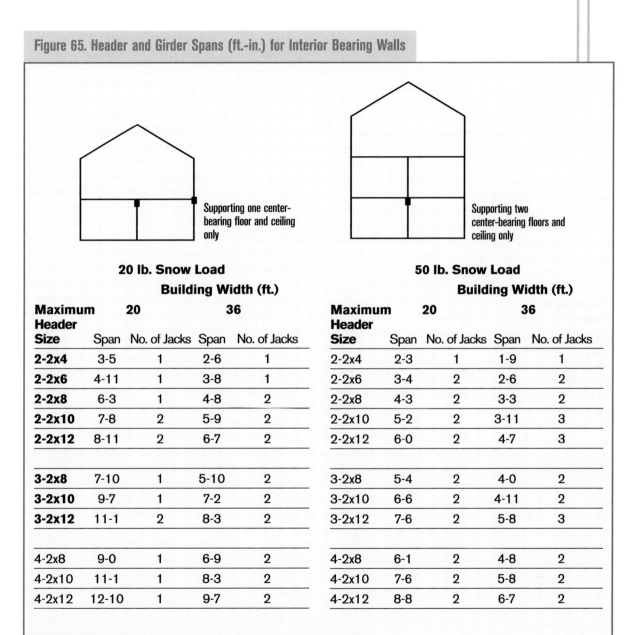

Supporting one center-bearing floor and ceiling only

Supporting two center-bearing floors and ceiling only

20 lb. Snow Load
Building Width (ft.)

Maximum Header Size	20 Span	No. of Jacks	36 Span	No. of Jacks
2-2x4	3-5	1	2-6	1
2-2x6	4-11	1	3-8	1
2-2x8	6-3	1	4-8	2
2-2x10	7-8	2	5-9	2
2-2x12	8-11	2	6-7	2
3-2x8	7-10	1	5-10	2
3-2x10	9-7	1	7-2	2
3-2x12	11-1	2	8-3	2
4-2x8	9-0	1	6-9	2
4-2x10	11-1	1	8-3	2
4-2x12	12-10	1	9-7	2

50 lb. Snow Load
Building Width (ft.)

Maximum Header Size	20 Span	No. of Jacks	36 Span	No. of Jacks
2-2x4	2-3	1	1-9	1
2-2x6	3-4	2	2-6	2
2-2x8	4-3	2	3-3	2
2-2x10	5-2	2	3-11	3
2-2x12	6-0	2	4-7	3
3-2x8	5-4	2	4-0	2
3-2x10	6-6	2	4-11	2
3-2x12	7-6	2	5-8	3
4-2x8	6-1	2	4-8	2
4-2x10	7-6	2	5-8	2
4-2x12	8-8	2	6-7	2

Note: Calculated spans assume #2 grade Doug.-Fir, Hem-Fir and SYP lumber.

Figure 69. Maximum Allowable Horizontal Spans (ft.-in.)

Rafters: 20 psf live load; 10 psf dead load. Non-snow region. Lightweight roof covering. No ceiling drywall.

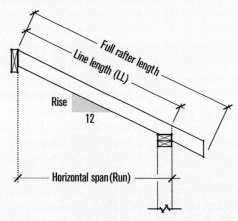

Species Group	Spacing (in.)	2x4 No. 1	2x4 No. 2	2x4 No. 1-2 (Can.)	2x6 No. 1	2x6 No. 2	2x6 No. 1-2 (Can.)	2x8 No. 1	2x8 No. 2	2x8 No. 1-2 (Can.)	2x10 No. 1	2x10 No. 2	2x10 No. 1-2 (Can.)
D-Fir-L	12	11-1	10-10	10-10	17-4	16-10	16-4	22-5	21-4	20-8	27-5	26-0	25-3
	16	10-0	9-10	9-8	15-4	14-7	14-2	19-5	18-5	17-11	23-9	22-6	21-11
	24	8-7	8-2	7-11	12-6	11-11	11-7	15-10	15-1	14-8	19-5	18-5	17-10
SPF	12	–	–	10-4	–	–	16-3	–	–	21-0	–	–	25-8
	16	–	–	9-5	–	–	14-4	–	–	18-2	–	–	22-3
	24	–	–	8-0	–	–	11-9	–	–	14-10	–	–	18-2
Hem-Fir	12	10-7	10-1	10-10	16-8	15-11	17-0	21-11	20-8	22-5	27-1	25-3	27-5
	16	9-8	9-2	9-10	15-2	14-2	15-4	19-2	17-11	19-5	23-5	21-11	23-9
	24	8-5	7-11	8-7	12-4	11-7	12-6	15-8	14-8	15-10	19-2	17-10	19-5
SYP	12	11-1	10-10	–	17-4	17-0	–	22-11	22-5	–	29-2	26-9	–
	16	10-0	9-10	–	15-9	15-1	–	20-10	19-6	–	25-10	23-2	–
	24	8-9	8-7	–	13-9	12-4	–	17-9	15-11	–	21-1	18-11	–

Figure 70. Maximum Allowable Horizontal Spans (ft.-in.)

Rafters: 20 psf live load; 10 psf dead load. Non-snow region. Light-weight roof covering. Drywall ceiling. No Attic.

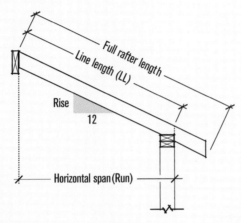

Species Group	Spacing (in.)	2x6 No. 1	2x6 No. 2	2x6 No. 1-2 (Can.)	2x8 No. 1	2x8 No. 2	2x8 No. 1-2 (Can.)	2x10 No. 1	2x10 No. 2	2x10 No. 1-2 (Can.)	2x12 No. 1	2x12 No. 2	2x12 No. 1-2 (Can.)
D-Fir-L	12	15-9	15-6	15-6	20-10	20-5	20-5	26-6	26-0	25-3	31-10	30-2	29-4
	16	14-4	14-1	14-1	18-11	18-5	17-11	23-9	22-6	21-11	27-6	26-1	25-5
	24	12-6	11-11	11-7	15-10	15-1	14-8	19-5	18-5	17-10	22-6	21-4	20-9
SPF	12	–	–	14-9	–	–	19-6	–	–	24-10	–	–	29-9
	16	–	–	13-5	–	–	17-9	–	–	22-3	–	–	25-9
	24	–	–	11-9	–	–	14-10	–	–	18-2	–	–	21-0
Hem-Fir	12	15-2	14-5	15-6	19-11	19-0	20-5	25-5	24-3	26-0	30-11	29-4	31-8
	16	13-9	13-1	14-1	18-2	17-3	18-6	23-2	21-11	23-8	27-2	25-5	27-6
	24	12-0	11-5	12-3	15-8	14-8	15-10	19-2	17-10	19-5	22-2	20-9	22-6
SYP	12	15-9	15-6	–	20-10	20-5	–	26-6	26-0	–	32-3	31-4	–
	16	14-4	14-1	–	18-11	18-6	–	24-1	23-2	–	29-4	27-2	–
	24	12-6	12-3	–	16-6	15-11	–	21-1	18-11	–	25-2	22-2	–

Figure 71. Maximum Allowable Horizontal Spans (ft.-in.)

Rafters: 20 psf live load; 10 psf dead load. Snow region. Light-weight roof covering. No ceiling drywall.

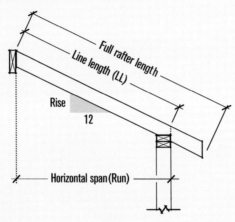

Species Group	Spacing (in.)	2x4			2x6			2x8			2x10		
		No. 1	No. 2	No. 1-2 (Can.)	No. 1	No. 2	No. 1-2 (Can.)	No. 1	No. 2	No. 1-2 (Can.)	No. 1	No. 2	No. 1-2 (Can.)
D-Fir-L	12	11-1	10-10	10-9	17-0	16-2	15-8	21-6	20-5	19-10	26-4	24-11	24-3
	16	10-0	9-7	9-3	14-9	14-0	13-7	18-8	17-8	17-2	22-9	21-7	21-0
	24	8-3	7-10	7-7	12-0	11-5	11-1	15-3	14-5	14-0	18-7	17-8	17-2
SPF	12	–	–	10-4	–	–	15-11	–	–	20-2	–	–	24-7
	16	–	–	9-5	–	–	13-9	–	–	17-5	–	–	21-4
	24	–	–	7-8	–	–	11-3	–	–	14-3	–	–	17-5
Hem-Fir	12	10-7	10-1	10-10	16-8	15-8	17-0	21-3	19-10	21-6	26-0	24-3	26-4
	16	9-8	9-2	9-10	14-6	13-7	14-9	18-5	17-2	18-8	22-6	21-0	22-9
	24	8-1	7-7	8-3	11-10	11-1	12-0	15-0	14-0	15-3	18-4	17-2	18-7
SYP	12	11-1	10-10	–	17-4	16-8	–	22-11	21-7	–	28-7	25-8	–
	16	10-0	9-10	–	15-9	14-5	–	20-10	18-8	–	24-9	22-3	–
	24	8-9	8-2	–	13-6	11-9	–	17-0	15-3	–	20-3	18-2	–

Figure 72. Maximum Allowable Horizontal Spans (ft.-in.)

Rafters: 20 psf live load; 10 psf dead load. Snow region. Lightweight roof covering. Drywall ceiling. No Attic.

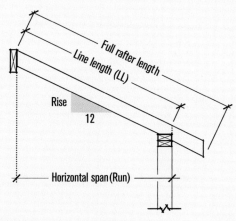

Species Group	Spacing (in.)	2x6 No. 1	2x6 No. 2	2x6 No. 1-2 (Can.)	2x8 No. 1	2x8 No. 2	2x8 No. 1-2 (Can.)	2x10 No. 1	2x10 No. 2	2x10 No. 1-2 (Can.)	2x12 No. 1	2x12 No. 2	2x12 No. 1-2 (Can.)
D-Fir-L	12	15-9	15-6	15-6	20-10	20-5	19-10	26-4	24-11	24-3	30-6	28-11	28-1
	16	14-4	14-0	13-7	18-8	17-8	17-2	22-9	21-7	21-0	26-5	25-1	24-4
	24	12-0	11-5	11-1	15-3	14-5	14-0	18-7	17-8	17-2	21-7	20-5	19-11
SPF	12	–	–	14-9	–	–	19-6	–	–	24-7	–	–	28-6
	16	–	–	13-5	–	–	17-5	–	–	21-4	–	–	24-8
	24	–	–	11-3	–	–	14-3	–	–	17-5	–	–	20-2
Hem-Fir	12	15-2	14-5	15-6	19-11	19-0	20-5	25-5	24-3	26-0	30-1	28-1	30-6
	16	13-9	13-1	14-1	18-2	17-2	18-6	22-6	21-0	22-9	26-1	24-4	26-5
	24	11-10	11-1	12-0	15-0	14-0	15-3	18-4	17-2	18-7	21-3	19-11	21-7
SYP	12	15-9	15-6	–	20-10	20-5	–	26-6	25-8	–	32-3	30-1	–
	16	14-4	14-1	–	18-11	18-6	–	24-1	22-3	–	29-4	26-1	–
	24	12-6	11-9	–	16-6	15-3	–	20-3	18-2	–	24-1	21-4	–

Figure 73. Maximum Allowable Horizontal Spans (ft.-in.)

Rafters: 30 psf live load; 10 psf dead load. Snow region. Lightweight roof covering. No ceiling drywall.

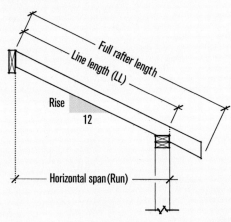

Species Group	Spacing (in.)	2x4			2x6			2x8			2x10		
		No. 1	No. 2	No. 1-2 (Can.)	No. 1	No. 2	No. 1-2 (Can.)	No. 1	No. 2	No. 1-2 (Can.)	No. 1	No. 2	No. 1-2 (Can.)
D-Fir-L	12	9-8	9-6	9-3	14-9	14-0	13-7	18-8	17-8	17-2	22-9	21-7	21-0
	16	8-9	8-3	8-0	12-9	12-1	11-9	16-2	15-4	14-11	19-9	18-9	18-2
	24	7-1	6-9	6-7	10-5	9-10	9-7	13-2	12-6	12-2	16-1	15-3	14-10
SPF	12	–	–	9-1	–	–	13-9	–	–	17-5	–	–	21-4
	16	–	–	8-2	–	–	11-11	–	–	15-1	–	–	18-5
	24	–	–	6-8	–	–	9-9	–	–	12-4	–	–	15-1
Hem-Fir	12	9-3	8-10	9-6	14-6	13-7	14-9	18-5	17-2	18-8	22-6	21-0	22-9
	16	8-5	8-0	8-7	12-7	11-9	12-9	15-11	14-11	16-2	19-6	18-2	19-9
	24	7-0	6-7	7-1	10-3	9-7	10-5	13-0	12-2	13-2	15-11	14-10	16-1
SYP	12	9-8	9-6	–	15-2	14-5	–	20-0	18-8	–	24-9	22-3	–
	16	8-9	8-7	–	13-9	12-6	–	18-0	16-2	–	21-5	19-3	–
	24	7-8	7-1	–	11-9	10-2	–	14-9	13-2	–	17-6	15-9	–

Figure 74. Maximum Allowable Horizontal Spans (ft.-in.)

Rafters: 30 psf live load; 10 psf dead load. Snow region. Lightweight roof covering. Drywall ceiling. No Attic.

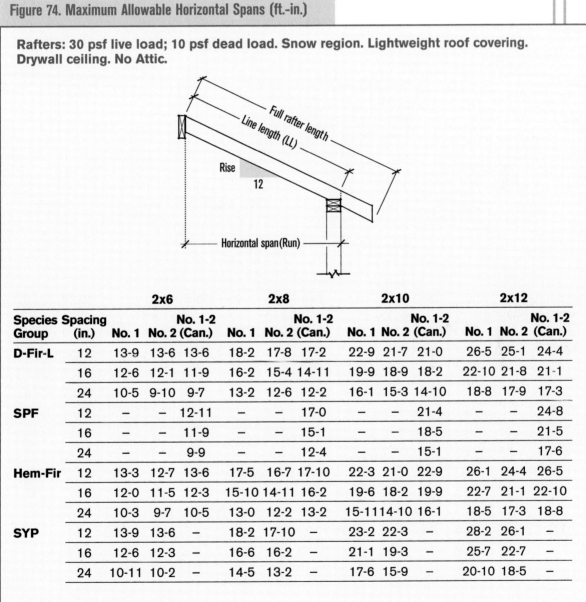

Species Group	Spacing (in.)	2x6			2x8			2x10			2x12		
		No. 1	No. 2	No. 1-2 (Can.)	No. 1	No. 2	No. 1-2 (Can.)	No. 1	No. 2	No. 1-2 (Can.)	No. 1	No. 2	No. 1-2 (Can.)
D-Fir-L	12	13-9	13-6	13-6	18-2	17-8	17-2	22-9	21-7	21-0	26-5	25-1	24-4
	16	12-6	12-1	11-9	16-2	15-4	14-11	19-9	18-9	18-2	22-10	21-8	21-1
	24	10-5	9-10	9-7	13-2	12-6	12-2	16-1	15-3	14-10	18-8	17-9	17-3
SPF	12	–	–	12-11	–	–	17-0	–	–	21-4	–	–	24-8
	16	–	–	11-9	–	–	15-1	–	–	18-5	–	–	21-5
	24	–	–	9-9	–	–	12-4	–	–	15-1	–	–	17-6
Hem-Fir	12	13-3	12-7	13-6	17-5	16-7	17-10	22-3	21-0	22-9	26-1	24-4	26-5
	16	12-0	11-5	12-3	15-10	14-11	16-2	19-6	18-2	19-9	22-7	21-1	22-10
	24	10-3	9-7	10-5	13-0	12-2	13-2	15-11	14-10	16-1	18-5	17-3	18-8
SYP	12	13-9	13-6	–	18-2	17-10	–	23-2	22-3	–	28-2	26-1	–
	16	12-6	12-3	–	16-6	16-2	–	21-1	19-3	–	25-7	22-7	–
	24	10-11	10-2	–	14-5	13-2	–	17-6	15-9	–	20-10	18-5	–

Figure 75. Maximum Allowable Horizontal Spans (ft.-in.)

Rafters: 30 psf live load; 20 psf dead load. Snow region. Heavy roof covering. No ceiling drywall.

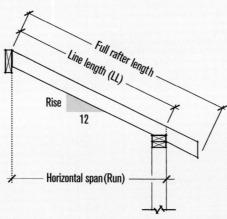

Species Group	Spacing (in.)	2x4 No. 1	2x4 No. 2	2x4 No. 1-2 (Can.)	2x6 No. 1	2x6 No. 2	2x6 No. 1-2 (Can.)	2x8 No. 1	2x8 No. 2	2x8 No. 1-2 (Can.)	2x10 No. 1	2x10 No. 2	2x10 No. 1-2 (Can.)
D-Fir-L	12	9-0	8-6	8-4	13-2	12-6	12-2	16-8	15-10	15-4	20-4	19-4	18-9
	16	7-10	7-5	7-2	11-5	10-10	10-6	14-5	13-8	13-4	17-8	16-9	16-3
	24	6-4	6-0	5-10	9-4	8-10	8-7	11-9	11-2	10-10	14-5	13-8	13-3
SPF	12	–	–	8-5	–	–	12-4	–	–	15-7	–	–	19-1
	16	–	–	7-3	–	–	10-8	–	–	13-6	–	–	16-6
	24	–	–	5-11	–	–	8-9	–	–	11-0	–	–	13-6
Hem-Fir	12	8-11	8-4	9-0	13-0	12-2	13-2	16-6	15-4	16-8	20-1	18-9	20-4
	16	7-8	7-2	7-10	11-3	10-6	11-5	14-3	13-4	14-5	17-5	16-3	17-8
	24	6-3	5-10	6-4	9-2	8-7	9-4	11-8	10-10	11-9	14-3	13-3	14-5
SYP	12	9-8	9-0	–	14-10	12-11	–	18-8	16-8	–	22-2	19-11	–
	16	8-8	7-9	–	12-10	11-2	–	16-2	14-5	–	19-2	17-3	–
	24	7-1	6-4	–	10-6	9-1	–	13-2	11-10	–	15-8	14-1	–

Figure 76. Maximum Allowable Horizontal Spans (ft.-in.)

Rafters: 30 psf live load; 20 psf dead load. Snow region. Heavy roof covering. Drywall ceiling. No Attic.

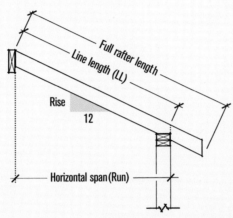

Species Group	Spacing (in.)	2x6 No. 1	2x6 No. 2	2x6 No. 1-2 (Can.)	2x8 No. 1	2x8 No. 2	2x8 No. 1-2 (Can.)	2x10 No. 1	2x10 No. 2	2x10 No. 1-2 (Can.)	2x12 No. 1	2x12 No. 2	2x12 No. 1-2 (Can.)
D-Fir-L	12	13-2	12-6	12-2	16-8	15-10	15-4	20-4	19-4	18-9	23-7	22-5	21-9
	16	11-5	10-10	10-6	14-5	13-8	13-4	17-8	16-9	16-3	20-5	19-5	18-10
	24	9-4	8-10	8-7	11-9	11-2	10-10	14-5	13-8	13-3	16-8	15-10	15-5
SPF	12	–	–	12-4	–	–	15-7	–	–	19-1	–	–	22-1
	16	–	–	10-8	–	–	13-6	–	–	16-6	–	–	19-2
	24	–	–	8-9	–	–	11-0	–	–	13-6	–	–	15-7
Hem-Fir	12	13-0	12-2	13-2	16-6	15-4	16-8	20-1	18-9	20-4	23-4	21-9	23-7
	16	11-3	10-6	11-5	14-3	13-4	14-5	17-5	16-3	17-8	20-2	18-10	20-5
	24	9-2	8-7	9-4	11-8	10-10	11-9	14-3	13-3	14-5	16-6	15-5	16-8
SYP	12	13-9	12-11	–	18-2	16-8	–	22-2	19-11	–	26-5	23-4	–
	16	12-6	11-2	–	16-2	14-5	–	19-2	17-3	–	22-10	20-2	–
	24	10-6	9-1	–	13-2	11-10	–	15-8	14-1	–	18-8	16-6	–

Figure 77. Maximum Allowable Horizontal Spans (ft.-in.)

Rafters: 40 psf live load; 10 psf dead load. Snow-region. Lightweight roof covering. No ceiling drywall.

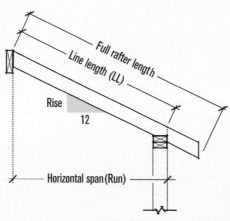

Species Group	Spacing (in.)	2x4 No. 1	2x4 No. 2	2x4 No. 1-2 (Can.)	2x6 No. 1	2x6 No. 2	2x6 No. 1-2 (Can.)	2x8 No. 1	2x8 No. 2	2x8 No. 1-2 (Can.)	2x10 No. 1	2x10 No. 2	2x10 No. 1-2 (Can.)
D-Fir-L	12	8-9	8-6	8-4	13-2	12-6	12-2	16-8	15-10	15-4	20-4	19-4	18-9
	16	7-10	7-5	7-2	11-5	10-10	10-6	14-5	13-8	13-4	17-8	16-9	16-3
	24	6-4	6-0	5-10	9-4	8-10	8-7	11-9	11-2	10-10	14-5	13-8	13-3
SPF	12	–	–	8-3	–	–	12-4	–	–	15-7	–	–	19-1
	16	–	–	7-3	–	–	10-8	–	–	13-6	–	–	16-6
	24	–	–	5-11	–	–	8-9	–	–	11-0	–	–	13-6
Hem-Fir	12	8-5	8-0	8-7	13-0	12-2	13-2	16-6	15-4	16-8	20-1	18-9	20-4
	16	7-8	7-2	7-10	11-3	10-6	11-5	14-3	13-4	14-5	17-5	16-3	17-8
	24	6-3	5-10	6-4	9-2	8-7	9-4	11-8	10-10	11-9	14-3	13-3	14-5
SYP	12	8-9	8-7	–	13-9	12-11	–	18-2	16-8	–	22-2	19-11	–
	16	8-0	7-9	–	12-6	11-2	–	16-2	14-5	–	19-2	17-3	–
	24	7-0	6-4	–	10-6	9-1	–	13-2	11-10	–	15-8	14-1	–

Figure 78. Maximum Allowable Horizontal Spans (ft.-in.)

Rafters: 40 psf live load; 10 psf dead load. Snow region. Lightweight roof covering. Drywall ceiling. No Attic.

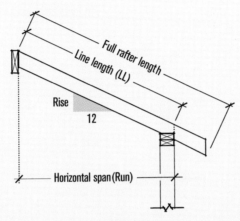

Species Group	Spacing (in.)	2x6			2x8			2x10			2x12		
		No. 1	No. 2	No. 1-2 (Can.)	No. 1	No. 2	No. 1-2 (Can.)	No. 1	No. 2	No. 1-2 (Can.)	No. 1	No. 2	No. 1-2 (Can.)
D-Fir-L	12	12-6	12-3	12-2	16-6	15-10	15-4	20-4	19-4	18-9	23-7	22-5	21-9
	16	11-5	10-10	10-6	14-5	13-8	13-4	17-8	16-9	16-3	20-5	19-5	18-10
	24	9-4	8-10	8-7	11-9	11-2	10-10	14-5	13-8	13-3	16-8	15-10	15-5
SPF	12	–	–	11-9	–	–	15-6	–	–	19-1	–	–	22-1
	16	–	–	10-8	–	–	13-6	–	–	16-6	–	–	19-2
	24	–	–	8-9	–	–	11-0	–	–	13-6	–	–	15-7
Hem-Fir	12	12-0	11-5	12-3	15-10	15-1	16-2	20-1	18-9	20-4	23-4	21-9	23-7
	16	10-11	10-5	11-2	14-3	13-4	14-5	17-5	16-3	17-8	20-2	18-10	20-5
	24	9-2	8-7	9-4	11-8	10-10	11-9	14-3	13-3	14-5	16-6	15-5	16-8
SYP	12	12-6	12-3	–	16-6	16-2	–	21-1	19-11	–	25-7	23-4	–
	16	11-5	11-2	–	15-0	14-5	–	19-2	17-3	–	22-10	20-2	–
	24	9-11	9-1	–	13-1	11-10	–	15-8	14-1	–	18-8	16-6	–

Figure 79. Maximum Allowable Horizontal Spans (ft.-in.)

Rafters: 40 psf live load; 15 psf dead load. Snow region. Medium-weight roof covering. No ceiling drywall.

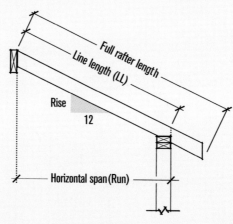

Species Group	Spacing (in.)	2x4			2x6			2x8			2x10		
		No. 1	No. 2	No. 1-2 (Can.)	No. 1	No. 2	No. 1-2 (Can.)	No. 1	No. 2	No. 1-2 (Can.)	No. 1	No. 2	No. 1-2 (Can.)
D-Fir-L	12	8-7	8-2	7-11	12-7	11-11	11-7	15-11	15-1	14-8	19-5	18-5	17-11
	16	7-5	7-1	6-10	10-10	10-4	10-0	13-9	13-1	12-8	16-10	15-11	15-6
	24	6-1	5-9	5-7	8-11	8-5	8-2	11-3	10-8	10-4	13-9	13-0	12-8
SPF	12	–	–	8-0	–	–	11-9	–	–	14-10	–	–	18-2
	16	–	–	6-11	–	–	10-2	–	–	12-11	–	–	15-9
	24	–	–	5-8	–	–	8-4	–	–	10-6	–	–	12-10
Hem-Fir	12	8-5	7-11	8-7	12-5	11-7	12-7	15-8	14-8	15-11	19-2	17-11	19-5
	16	7-4	6-10	7-5	10-9	10-0	10-10	13-7	12-8	13-9	16-7	15-6	16-10
	24	6-0	5-7	6-1	8-9	8-2	8-11	11-1	10-4	11-3	13-7	12-8	13-9
SYP	12	8-9	8-7	–	13-9	12-4	–	17-9	15-11	–	21-1	19-0	–
	16	8-0	7-5	–	12-3	10-8	–	15-5	13-9	–	18-3	16-5	–
	24	6-9	6-1	–	10-0	8-8	–	12-7	11-3	–	14-11	13-5	–

Figure 80. Maximum Allowable Horizontal Spans (ft.-in.)

Rafters: 40 psf live load; 15 psf dead load. Snow region. Medium-weight roof covering. Drywall ceiling. No Attic.

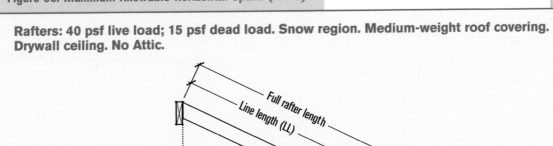

Species Group	Spacing (in.)	2x6 No. 1	2x6 No. 2	2x6 No. 1-2 (Can.)	2x8 No. 1	2x8 No. 2	2x8 No. 1-2 (Can.)	2x10 No. 1	2x10 No. 2	2x10 No. 1-2 (Can.)	2x12 No. 1	2x12 No. 2	2x12 No. 1-2 (Can.)
D-Fir-L	12	12-6	11-11	11-7	15-11	15-1	14-8	19-5	18-5	17-11	22-6	21-4	20-9
	16	10-10	10-4	10-0	13-9	13-1	12-8	16-10	15-11	15-6	19-6	18-6	18-0
	24	8-11	8-5	8-2	11-3	10-8	10-4	13-9	13-0	12-8	15-11	15-1	14-8
SPF	12	–	–	11-9	–	–	14-10	–	–	18-2	–	–	21-1
	16	–	–	10-2	–	–	12-11	–	–	15-9	–	–	18-3
	24	–	–	8-4	–	–	10-6	–	–	12-10	–	–	14-11
Hem-Fir	12	12-0	11-5	12-3	15-8	14-8	15-11	19-2	17-11	19-5	22-3	20-9	22-6
	16	10-9	10-0	10-10	13-7	12-8	13-9	16-7	15-6	16-10	19-3	18-0	19-6
	24	8-9	8-2	8-11	11-1	10-4	11-3	13-7	12-8	13-9	15-9	14-8	15-11
SYP	12	12-6	12-3	–	16-6	15-11	–	21-1	19-0	–	25-2	22-3	–
	16	11-5	10-8	–	15-0	13-9	–	18-3	16-5	–	21-9	19-3	–
	24	9-11	8-8	–	12-7	11-3	–	14-11	13-5	–	17-9	15-9	–

Figure 81. Maximum Allowable Horizontal Spans (ft.-in.)

Rafters: 50 psf live load; 10 psf dead load. Snow region. Lightweight roof covering. Drywall ceiling. No Attic.

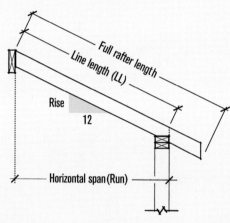

Species Group	Spacing (in.)	2x6			2x8			2x10			2x12		
		No. 1	No. 2	No. 1-2 (Can.)	No. 1	No. 2	No. 1-2 (Can.)	No. 1	No. 2	No. 1-2 (Can.)	No. 1	No. 2	No. 1-2 (Can.)
D-Fir-L	12	11-8	11-5	11-1	15-3	14-5	14-0	18-7	17-8	17-2	21-7	20-5	19-11
	16	10-5	9-10	9-7	13-2	12-6	12-2	16-1	15-3	14-10	18-8	17-9	17-3
	24	8-6	8-1	7-10	10-9	10-3	9-11	13-2	12-6	12-1	15-3	14-6	14-1
SPF	12	–	–	10-11	–	–	14-3	–	–	17-5	–	–	20-2
	16	–	–	9-9	–	–	12-4	–	–	15-1	–	–	17-6
	24	–	–	7-11	–	–	10-1	–	–	12-4	–	–	14-3
Hem-Fir	12	11-2	10-8	11-5	14-8	14-0	15-0	18-4	17-2	18-7	21-3	19-11	21-7
	16	10-2	9-7	10-4	13-0	12-2	13-2	15-11	14-10	16-1	18-5	17-3	18-8
	24	8-5	7-10	8-6	10-8	9-11	10-9	13-0	12-1	13-2	15-1	14-1	15-3
SYP	12	11-8	11-5	–	15-4	15-0	–	19-7	18-2	–	23-9	21-4	–
	16	10-7	10-2	–	13-11	13-2	–	17-6	15-9	–	20-10	18-5	–
	24	9-3	8-4	–	12-0	10-9	–	14-4	12-10	–	17-0	15-1	–

Figure 82. Maximum Allowable Horizontal Spans (ft.-in.)

Rafters: 50 psf live load; 15 psf dead load. Snow region. Medium-weight roof covering. Drywall ceiling. No Attic.

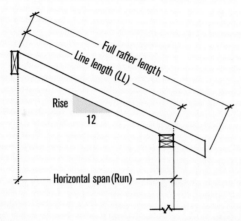

Species Group	Spacing (in.)	2x6 No. 1	2x6 No. 2	2x6 No. 1-2 (Can.)	2x8 No. 1	2x8 No. 2	2x8 No. 1-2 (Can.)	2x10 No. 1	2x10 No. 2	2x10 No. 1-2 (Can.)	2x12 No. 1	2x12 No. 2	2x12 No. 1-2 (Can.)
D-Fir-L	12	11-7	10-11	10-8	14-7	13-10	13-6	17-10	16-11	16-6	20-9	19-8	19-1
	16	10-0	9-6	9-3	12-8	12-0	11-8	15-6	14-8	14-3	17-11	17-0	16-6
	24	8-2	7-9	7-6	10-4	9-10	9-6	12-8	12-0	11-8	14-8	13-11	13-6
SPF	12	–	–	10-10	–	–	13-8	–	–	16-9	–	–	19-5
	16	–	–	9-4	–	–	11-10	–	–	14-6	–	–	16-9
	24	–	–	7-8	–	–	9-8	–	–	11-10	–	–	13-8
Hem-Fir	12	11-2	10-8	11-5	14-5	13-6	14-7	17-8	16-6	17-10	20-5	19-1	20-9
	16	9-10	9-3	10-0	12-6	11-8	12-8	15-3	14-3	15-6	17-9	16-6	17-11
	24	8-1	7-6	8-2	10-3	9-6	10-4	12-6	11-8	12-8	14-6	13-6	14-8
SYP	12	11-8	11-4	–	15-4	14-8	–	19-5	17-6	–	23-2	20-6	–
	16	10-7	9-10	–	13-11	12-8	–	16-10	15-1	–	20-0	17-9	–
	24	9-2	8-0	–	11-7	10-4	–	13-9	12-4	–	16-4	14-6	–